D0457006

Dear Mister Essay Writer Guy

Dear
MISTER ESSAY
WRITER GUY

Advice and Confessions on
Writing, Love, and Cannibals

Dinty W. Moore

TEN SPEED PRESS
Berkeley

To the

Polar Bears.

Be gentle with me.

CONTENTS

"Is Truth stranger than Fiction? This is a question that has half the world at loggerheads and the other half at sixes and sevens."
—ROBERT BENCHLEY

"What do I know?"
—MICHEL DE MONTAIGNE

INTRODUCTION

Perhaps you are standing in the bookstore, scanning this introductory chapter, wondering just what sort of book you have in hand. You are a good-looking person whose minor flaws seem to only accentuate your considerable charm. You are intelligent. And immune to flattery.

Moreover, you admire those who are plain-spoken, so let me be entirely forthright:

This is the most important book ever published, except for a very old book that Moses started writing back in 800 BCE, one that a bunch of saints and raggedy disciples had to finish for him over the next thousand years.

Talk about missing a deadline! Boy, *his* editor must have been mighty ticked off.

In any case, that other book is all well and good, but it rapidly bogs down in questions such as how many goats must be slaughtered to atone for beheading your eldest son and who begat whom.

Good stuff if you are a theologian, but stop to think a moment: are you a theologian?

Probably not.

The book you are holding here tackles more urgent questions, questions more relevant to the modern reader, questions such as "What is the essay? And why? And how ought we to feel about it, given that there is nothing on television this evening?"

To that end, I have reached out to contemporary essayists such as Phillip Lopate, Cheryl Strayed, Diane Ackerman, Lee Gutkind, Steve Almond, Lia Purpura, Ander Monson, and a host of other fine writers, many of whom are close friends with Oprah Winfrey. I asked each of them to send me a question about the contemporary essay, in an attempt to once and for all settle the burning question: who reads this stuff?

My inspiration here is the sixteenth-century French nobleman and father of the essay form Michel de Montaigne. He broke literary ground by writing mainly of the self, bravely admitting to the reader, "I cannot keep my subject still. It goes along befuddled and staggering, with a natural drunkenness."

Drunkenness, befuddlement, the occasional staggering. What's not to like?

For those of you who have wondered, by the way, the name Montaigne is pronounced this way: Montaigne.

So this is a Writing Guide of sorts, but since the true arc of the essay is the author's thoughts moving on the page in a compelling fashion, this is also a Thinking Guide. If you have trouble thinking, this is the book for you!

Enjoy yourself. Consider reading passages aloud to your spouse or partner, or just slither up to a complete stranger at the corner coffee shop and let loose a chapter or two. You'll find yourself making lifelong friends that way.

And afterward, if you have questions, or are wondering where to send flowers, feel free to contact me (misteressayguy@gmail.com). I do so look forward to hearing from you.

Sincerely,

Dinty W. Moore
aka Mister Essay Writer Guy

A Question from
PHILLIP LOPATE

Mister Essay Writer GUY

Dear Mister Essay Writer Guy,

I am curious how you deal honestly with male-female relations in general and specifically your past girlfriends on the page without coming off as a male chauvinist pig.

Looking for guidance,

Phillip Lopate
New York, New York

Dear Phillip,

What an excellent question. Do I have to answer it? Yes, I suppose I do, since you were kind enough to pose the question, and since I've decided to feature it as the first question in this book. It would be odd, I suppose, to just blow right by.

I believe the best way to avoid coming off as a male chauvinist pig might be to *not be* a male chauvinist pig? Is that a stretch? Another way might be to adopt a writing persona, perhaps one where you seem grateful, not vindictive or sour, and just vulnerable enough that the readers want to tuck you in and feed you soup.

I've written an essay, trying out my theory. I sipped a cup of warm broth as I wrote it. You might try that as well.

Yours, gratefully,

Mister Essay Writer Guy

Of Old Girlfriends

First of all, I am grateful.

And I wish there had been more of you.

But I fully understand.

***

As a young man, I was distant, frightened, and naïve. And I was a bit of a prig.

In retrospect, these are not traits that set a young girl's heart aflutter.

I had all of the usual longings, of course, in occasionally dazzling amounts, but was somehow convinced by the Catholic Church that these biological impulses were mere evidence of my inherent wickedness. Even now I'm at a loss to describe why other boys my age were able to deduce that the priests were spreading misinformed malarkey while I stupidly swallowed the fiction host, line, and sinker.

But that was me, the brooding and stupid one, ready to believe that the soft, scented body of a gentle young woman was somehow a bouquet of poison sumac.

My friends were less afflicted, and despite my confusion about women and love, I often tagged along on dates. My best friend in high school, Herkman, was a musician, and it was not uncommon for me to be tasked with keeping his girlfriend entertained while he fiddled with unreliable amplifiers, argued over chord progressions, smoked a little reefer in the keyboard player's van, and banged out a couple of sets on a Friday or Saturday evening. It was a classic division of labor. I chatted her up and made her laugh; later my friend Herkman French-kissed her in the back of the Buick Skylark and felt around a bit under her bra.

***

I had two girl friends in high school. There is, of course, an excruciating difference between *girlfriend* and *girl friend*.

One of my girl friends spoke to me on the phone for an hour almost every weeknight, and I was profoundly in love. Lisa and I would chat about books sometimes, but usually we discussed her boyfriend: a lump of a young man and a star wrestler.

"Do you think Matthew likes me?" she would ask halfway through every phone call. "Did he mention me at all in school today?"

I would answer honestly and earnestly, in detail, just to keep her on the line. If she heard my heart breaking, she probably thought it was just static.

My other girl friend, Mary Carole, had a screened-in back porch where she did her homework each afternoon, and once or twice a week I would ride my bike up her driveway and visit a while. She and I would discuss the fascinating, artsy lives we hoped to lead someday, and often her mother would bring us out some iced tea. But Mary Carole had boyfriends too, and they were also my classmates, and more often than not, I ended up in the role of matchmaker.

"Ronnie is so cute," she would say. "Don't you think?"

I didn't think. I just brooded.

Years later, at Mary Carole's wedding reception, her mother called to me across four rows of tables at the Waterford Fire Hall, "I still think she should've married you, Dinty."

Yeah, me too.

***

The high school I attended was named the Cathedral Preparatory School for Young Catholic Boys. It was a prep school, preparing us for one of two futures: either playing football or spending our lives getting sucker-punched by those who did play football.

The girls in town all went to Villa Maria High, where they chiefly learned how to use safety pins to adjust the hems of their skirts, depending on whether they were in school, on the city bus, or hanging out downtown waiting for the football players to walk by.

I'd like to think that this strict gender segregation contributed to my acute awkwardness—that if I had been in regular contact with young women my age, I would gradually have come to see them as human, accessible, similarly interested in exploring romance and budding sexuality.

Instead, I was convinced that they were young nuns in training, and that they would slap me—hard—like the nuns themselves, if they had even an inkling of what I wanted.

I wanted to see them naked, and touch them, and then kiss them. And then marry them and worship them forever.

Horrible stuff like that.

***

I went to two proms. The first—my junior year—I attended only because Lisa and Mary Carole insisted. They even chose my date, Maureen, an extremely nice young girl who for some reason didn't appeal to me in the slightest. For one thing, she was from the wealthy part of town, and I bitterly resented those kids. For another, she was deeply religious.

I should point out, for the sake of honesty and painful irony, that despite my total acceptance of the Catholic teachings on sexuality, I had pretty much rejected every other aspect of my assigned faith. I was the scourge of religion class, making the young priests earn their paltry wages by refuting my logical arguments against infallibility, original sin, virgin birth, and resurrection.

"If God *is* all-powerful," I'd ask Father Humenay, "why did He need Judas to betray Jesus? I mean, He could have done what He wanted without all the drama. I doubt that Judas actually had any choice about turning Jesus over to the Roman soldiers, not when *God's Entire Plan for the Universe* hinged on his decision!"

At this point, Father Humenay would have turned all red.

"Really, Father," I would say, throwing up my hands in mock confusion. "It makes no sense."

None of it made sense, actually. Except for that part about my filthy masculine impulses. That seemed spot on.

As for Maureen, it wouldn't have been nice to *not* ask her to the prom, given the onslaught of phone calls from Lisa and Mary Carole, along the lines of "Maureen is *really really* waiting for you to ask her."

Yes, along with all of my other unattractive traits, I was fastidiously polite. I didn't want to hurt Maureen's feelings. So I asked her, bought her a nice corsage, then treated her like an unwanted cousin all evening. No doubt I hurt her feelings more than if I hadn't called at all.

Two weeks before my *senior* prom, Eric, the keyboard player in my friend Herkman's band, broke up with his girlfriend, Laurie Lynn, whom I had loved from afar for months. Uncharacteristically, I found the guts to ask her to be my date, and amazingly, she accepted. I picked her up in my mother's green Plymouth Valiant, tried to think of clever things to say so she would laugh, and avoided holding her hand or dancing close in case she got the wrong impression about me.

In any case, by midnight, Laurie Lynn and Eric had spotted one another across the ballroom at Rainbow Gardens and said "I'm sorry" with their eyes.

By 1 a.m., she was in his van.

I have to assume she got home all right.

***

College was different.

The girls were older.

Stephanie was elfish, beautiful, whip-smart, and artistic, and I fell for her the moment we met. We dated, or hung out in a way I thought was dating, for most of my first semester, meaning we went to Marx Brothers or Woody Allen movies in the University of Pittsburgh student union, and then I walked her home, a good two miles into the residential center of Squirrel Hill. I loved those two miles and all the deep conversations we shared, and I especially enjoyed the modest kiss on her mother's porch before she slipped through the door.

One night in late December, though, after a Christmas party in a friend's apartment, Stephanie looked at the snow falling thickly around us, and said, "I'm too tired to walk. Why don't I stay in your room?"

I thought, "Yes!" and my heart raced. We slipped into my dorm, I gave her one of my big white T-shirts to wear in lieu of a nightgown, and then all night long I didn't touch her, brush up against her, breathe heavily in her direction, or let on that I was so erect I was about to have an untimely heart attack.

"If she sees what a gentleman I am, she'll fall so much in love she'll be mine forever," I reasoned.

Yes, I had that exact thought.

It would be hilarious if it weren't so pathetic.

Not too long after, she was sleeping with my best friend, Peter.

I couldn't blame them—though for about two years I did.

**

No, I am not still a virgin.

If I were, I wouldn't tell you. But I'm not.

There was a young lady named Shelly, my junior year of college, who hung around my office in the student newspaper suite for weeks, dropping subtle hints, then not-so-subtle hints, then hints that resembled large, hardwood tree trunks aimed at my thick forehead. Eventually, one thunderstormy Friday evening, she looked me directly in the eye and said, "You've never done this before, have you?"

I shook my head, smiling like a shy toddler.

She took matters into her own hands.

She was lovely.

To be honest, I'm not precisely sure if we grow wiser when we age or just begin to see more clearly how ridiculous we were in our youth.

Maybe it is all one and the same.

A Question from
CHERYL STRAYED

Mister Essay Writer Guy

Dear Mister Essay Writer Guy,

I have a hot crush on the em dash. Seldom can I write a paragraph—let alone a page!—that isn't riddled with these lovely marks of punctuation that allow me to either set aside or append a word or phrase. I've often wondered if this is a problem, and now I'm asking you, comrade-in-punctuation-quandaries. What does my need to stuff—while simultaneously fracturing—my sentences—with the meandering, the explanatory, the discursive, the perhaps not-entirely-necessary—say about me? And more importantly, what does it give to—or take away from—my work? Is it a quirk I should mindfully scale back? A bad habit I should lose? An original impulse that I should honor without restraint?

Yours,

Cheryl Strayed
Portland, Oregon

Dear Cheryl,

You do realize that 99 percent of the civilized world has no idea what an "em dash" is, right?

What I mean is, they probably think that the "em dash" is a benefit race for those fighting to cure mononucleosis.

Not that mononucleosis is any small thing. My friend Jackson had mono in junior high, and we all figured he got it from kissing some ninth-grader. He had to stay home for three months and watch television, which isn't so bad, but when he came back we teased him mercilessly. Today, a mature man in his midfifties, he wears a bad hairpiece and sometimes has spit bubbles in the corner of his mouth.

But I digress—as do you—which is the point.

The contemporary essayist, whom I am pledged to assist in any way possible, should indeed understand both grammar and punctuation. And if she wishes to interrupt herself, she should cough delicately, waiting for a polite pause, rather than barging right in.

I remain, Madam, your faithful and patient servant,

Mister Essay Writer Guy

Dash It All

A friend of mine asked me recently about the em dash, that peculiar bit of punctuation most people mistake for a hyphen. You have to be a bit of a punctuation nerd to even know that the em dash exists, and an even bigger grammar geek to know that there is both an em dash and an en dash, and they are not the same thing. But that's my friend—and that's me.

The hyphen is short. It is used to hyphenate words, such as shilly-shally.

One definition of shilly-shally is "to spend time on insignificant things."

Ahem.

The en dash is a bit longer than our friend the hyphen—about the width of an "n." This minute size distinction likely makes no sense to you, but it might have made sense to those folks who printed books and periodicals by casting lead type into galleys, roughly during the years 1450–1950.

That's how the en dash is most often used, by the way—to separate items that fall into ranges.

For instance, dates:

> Books and periodicals were cast in lead type roughly during the years 1450–1950.

Or,

> Being awkward, I had no dates during the period 1974–76.

The en dash is also suitable for other things that fall into ranges. Such as:

> There were roughly 40–50 young women I wanted to date, but I only had the nerve to ask two of them, and they both said "No."

And,

> So I was determined to be entirely unattractive, by a 2–0 vote.

You're getting the gist of this, yes?

***

Which brings us—finally—to the em dash—longer still, or about the width of an "m." In informal writing, em dashes can replace commas, semicolons, colons, the large intestine, and parentheses to indicate added emphasis, an interruption, or a change of thought.

One example:

> I have three goals for my day—measure an "n" and an "m," memorize the width of the two letters, and look up "obsessive disorders" on Wikipedia.

Or:

> Gutenberg—his full name was Johannes Gensfleisch zur Laden zum Gutenberg—invented mechanical movable type printing and thus started the Printing Revolution—which led directly to the proliferation of the written word—and thus led as well to the meditative essay, the commonplace essay, the lyric essay, and the humorous essay, as exhibited here. Had he

seen my essay coming, Gutenberg might have chosen to hide his invention in the basement.

***

Here's a fun fact:

Though Johannes Gutenberg gets credit for inventing the printing press, and thus the en and em dash, his delinquent great-nephew Otto von Daubenspeck Gutenberg is the one who invented the innovative "enemy dash"—a rare punctuation mark the width of an en, an em, and a y—used primarily to poke people in the face.

Like this:

 I may have just made that part up.

Yes, most certainly.

***

My friend who asked me about the em dash was not asking out of sheer perversity. This friend is a writer, of wonderful books, and known for her own advice column, Dear Sugar, which was inspired by *this* book, the one you hold in your hands right now, though oddly and amazingly she wrote her advice columns many years *before* this book was written.

Truth is stranger than fiction!

In any case, my friend wondered about the increasing use of the em dash in modern writing and how it might connect to shortened attention spans and the fracturing of image and idea in contemporary society.

Those are serious questions.

Let me avoid them as best I can.

Yes, the occasional—carefully measured and monitored—use of the em dash is a lovely thing to behold. Such—emphasis!

But more to the point, why wouldn't any young women agree to date me during the ages 19–21? I was average looking—well, I'm hardly objective on that topic, am I? —and I was funny—and—well, perhaps you don't want to hear any more about my ill-fated romantic life as a young man—and perhaps you think I am being maudlin—and by the way, maudlin is a fascinating word—it means excessively weepy or self-pitying—and is an alteration of Mary Magdalene—who is often portrayed in art as weeping—thus, maudlin—and who, by the way, probably would also have chosen not to date me—and another interesting connection is that Gutenberg's printing press helped to make Mary Magdalene famous, since Gutenberg mainly printed Bibles—Gutenberg Bibles!—though how he resisted the temptation to substitute his own name everywhere it said "God" is a mystery to me—he might have changed the world—and certainly would have spiked an upward trend in *his* dating life—Golly! I'm hungry!

As you have just observed, excessive use of the em dash can indeed be disruptive to the flow of a piece of writing.

So now my friend has her answer.

A Question from
JULIANNA BAGGOTT

Mister Essay Writer Guy

Dear Mister Essay Writer Guy,

I like to jot my essay ideas on cocktail napkins the way I believe it was done in days of yore. (Were not the initial ideas for *The Crack-Up* first jotted on a cocktail napkin? I have a hard time believing otherwise.) Alas, cocktail napkins are mostly found in bars, and I am a hypochondriac who fears not only sicknesses and diseases of various sorts but also a wide range of falls. In short, I don't want to become an alcoholic just because I want to be a writer. My question is multifold, like an accordion. A. Why does the history of writers seem to include so much alcoholism? B. Is it necessary? C. If I simply bought packets of cocktail napkins from a party supply store and jotted ideas at my kitchen table, would my writing still have that *je ne sais quoi*, as the French say? and possibly D. [depending on your knowledge of French language and culture] why do the French—who are great essayists—have an extremely popular phrase that's so empty and shruggy and vague? E. Aren't we supposed to write with detailed language and not just say "I don't know what"?

All my best,

Julianna Baggott
Tallahassee, Florida

Dear Ms. Baggott,

I don't know. What?

Sincerely,

Mister Essay Writer Guy

THE NAPKIN IS THE MESSAGE

by Dinty W. Moore

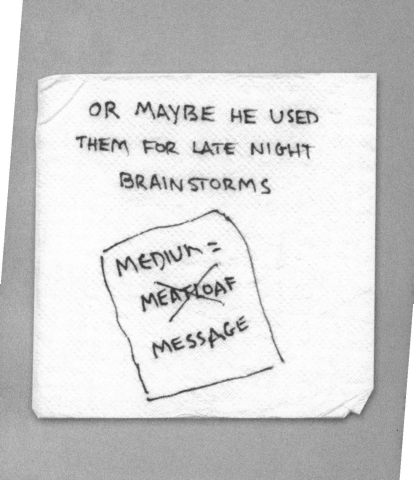

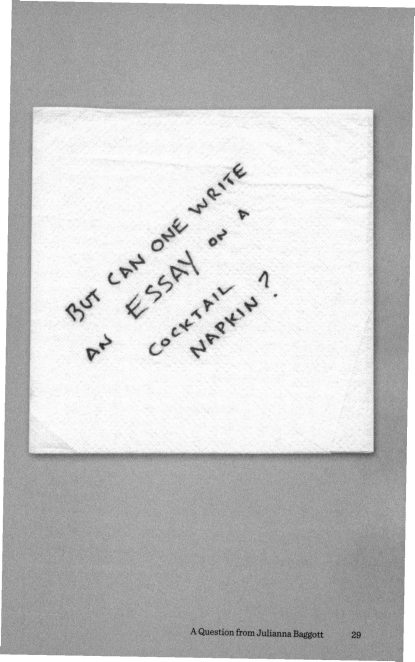

BUT CAN ONE WRITE
AN ESSAY ON A
COCKTAIL
NAPKIN ?

AND THE INK CAUSED A HORRIBLE MESS

McLUHAN FOCUSED NOT JUST ON HOW THE MEDIUM CHANGES THE MESSAGE, BUT ON HOW A NEW MEDIUM CHANGES US, THE MESSENGERS AND RECIPIENTS ...

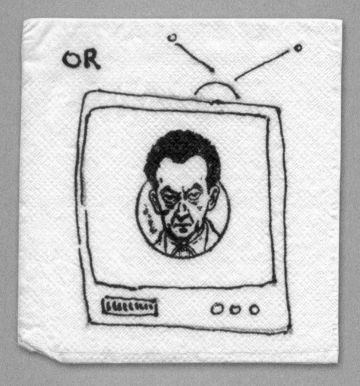

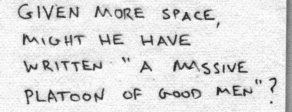

GIVEN MORE SPACE,
MIGHT HE HAVE
WRITTEN "A MASSIVE
PLATOON OF GOOD MEN"?

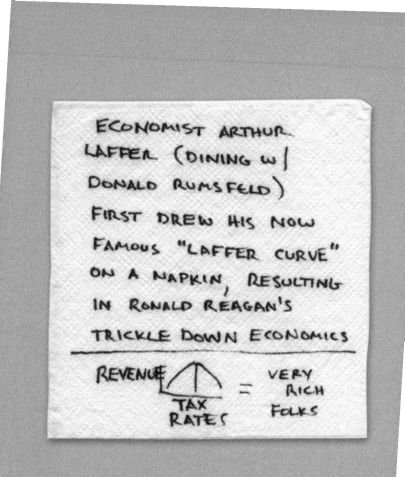

ECONOMIST ARTHUR LAFFER (DINING W/ DONALD RUMSFELD) FIRST DREW HIS NOW FAMOUS "LAFFER CURVE" ON A NAPKIN, RESULTING IN RONALD REAGAN'S TRICKLE DOWN ECONOMICS

REVENUE ⌢ = VERY RICH FOLKS

TAX RATES

BUT IF HE
HAD USED
HIS NAPKIN
PROPERLY,
THERE WOULD
HAVE BEEN
FAR LESS
TRICKLING!

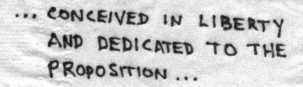

A Question from
JUDITH KITCHEN

Mister Essay Writer Guy

Dear Mister Essay Writer Guy,

The other night I was at a cocktail party and I was telling a story and the person I was telling the story to said, "You know, you really ought to write about that." So I jotted down some notes for what I would write and now, this morning, my notes don't make a whole lot of sense. There's something about how no two zebras' stripes are alike, sort of like our fingerprints, and I was talking about the one time I was fingerprinted and what I was feeling when they pushed my fingers down on that ink pad and rolled them from right to left over that paper. I mean, they did that for each finger and that seemed excessive to me—and I know I said that word ("excessive") when I was telling the story, but then in my notes it says something about a waterfall and there's something I can't read up in the left-hand corner where some wine made the ink blur, but maybe I can reconstruct that part if I ever do start writing. I think that since my story was true—for the most part—I really ought to write an essay, but I did kinda lie a bit at the end (just to make it work better and, well, the wine) and I'm wondering this: if I can figure out what my story was about, should I keep the good ending, or should I tell what really happened? I thought you might know because your endings always almost sound real. Another problem is that my story was funny (the wine again) and usually I'm a very serious person, so how do I recapture the humor without getting drunk? Also, just what is the difference between a story and an essay, because I've seen those terms used interchangeably, so do you have to have a "story" to be able to write an essay? I don't usually have any stories, just some random thoughts. Oh dear, I've gone on and on, but I can't think of which of my questions I should delete, so I'm just sending this. Thank you in advance. I read your column every time I read the newspaper, which is not as often as it used to be.

Sincerely—and hopefully—yours,

Judith Kitchen
Port Townsend, Washington

Dear Judith,

That's a lot of questions. Let me take them one at a time:

1. Don't lie. Nonfiction writers are obliged to use the true ending, not the more dramatic one.

2. You ask me how do you recapture the humor without getting drunk again? That just seems like a silly question. Why would you *not* want to get drunk again?

3. The difference between a story and an essay is that the storyteller just wants to entertain the reader, while the essayist has been to graduate school.

4. Funny you should mention zebras.

Honestly, thanks,

Mister Essay Writer Guy

A Striped Essay

I met my first zebra the summer I worked at the Erie Zoo as a replacement zookeeper. My duties included chopping apples and carrots for the elephant breakfast one week, thawing foul-smelling slabs of mystery meat for the lions a week later, and in the third week, throwing frozen mackerel across a wide moat to a pair of jaded polar bears. I was the fill-in: my assignment shifted according to which of the regular zookeeping staff was taking vacation.

In mid-July, my supervisor assigned me "up the hill, with the hoof stock" for the following week, and I was absolutely delighted. My new charges would include caring for the small zebra family, a group that had long fascinated me from afar. The alternating white and black stripes made the zebras seem almost magical, like an animal more from the Land of Oz than from Africa.

I had seen birds with majestic plumage, of course—the zoo had three peacocks, five flamingos, and a few exotic parrots—and I owned a small home aquarium with various tropical fish sporting unusual patterns, but such distinctive markings are rare in four-legged land animals. I was convinced that such a visually striking creature would be fascinating in close quarters.

And so Monday finally came, and I spent some time caring for the boldly banded mammal of my imagination. The zebras, it turned out, each and every one of them, were obstinate, smelly, and dull. Perhaps the dullest animals in the zoo.

The zoo had two world-weary horses—retired Clydesdales—but they, at least, would wander to the fence out of curiosity when I approached and, if I fed them a handful of grass and weeds, would flash their eyelashes in what seemed like gratitude. We had a hundred-year-old turtle that slept most of the day, but when he did wake up, he seemed wise and venerable, and the beak he used to chew his lettuce was fascinatingly prehistoric.

But the zebras?

No personality whatsoever.

They just chewed.

Stood there.

Chewed some more.

***

I *ate* my first zebra one summer evening just after I downed a pint of Bonnie Birdie Ale in the Thistle Street Bar, in Edinburgh, Scotland.

Specifically, I had a zebra burger.

I was in a foreign land, understand—not quite as foreign as Botswana, perhaps, where zebras roam the spacious grasslands in herds sometimes numbering in the thousands, but foreign enough. I had already tried some Scottish foods quite alien to my tongue: stargazy pie, blood pudding, neeps and tatties, cullen skink. What is travel good for if not new experiences?

So when I saw the shop just off Queen Street advertising zebra burgers, I checked my stomach sensors for signs of hunger, and what I heard back was a rumbling voice that seemed to say, *Try it out, old sport.*

I did, and, to be honest, I rather liked it.

The zebra burger offered a bit more chew and texture than the common American beef hamburger. Think of good steak, ground and mixed fifty-fifty with extremely lean pork. There was, in addition, more flavor than the American standard, a rich juiciness reminiscent of roast beef *au jus*. And a decidedly sweet aftertaste: an unexpected second wave of flavor.

I didn't need a drop of ketchup.

And that was that.

***

But it has been months now since I've returned, and on those occasions when I mention my unusual burger experience to friends, the response usually goes like this:

"You ate *what*?"

Often the voice will rise with each syllable, as if perhaps I had snuck onto the stage during a production of *The Lion King* and dragged my prey into the wings while children screamed, fainted, and ran madly up the aisles.

"Zebra? *Really*?"

The look in my friends' eyes is not one of admiration. Clearly, in the minds of many, I have crossed a line.

So, I ask myself, what did I eat, exactly?

A zebra is of the horse family, a close cousin to the wild ass. Zebras wander vast plains eating grass, much like the domestic cow.

Zebras are hard to domesticate and are not commonly kept as pets. Pigs are infinitely smarter, if that's our criteria.

But the zebra has stripes. Stripes seem exotic. Exotic reminds us of rhinoceros horn and panda bear, and we make a certain leap in our minds.

To endangered species.

Smuggling rings.

The truth, however, is that the zebra meat sold for human consumption in the United Kingdom is farm raised, like beef cattle, much of it right there in the UK.

Zebra herds—I'm speaking of the plains zebra here; there are a few rarer varieties— are for the most part doing just fine in their native African terrain. The global demand is very small, and fully sustainable.

So did I actually cross a line? Or just a stripe?

***

To be fully forthcoming, let me confess this:

I'm a bit ambivalent about eating creatures at all. We meat-eaters have learned too much about factory farms and animal consciousness, in my opinion, to remain blissfully naïve about our choices.

I still eat meat and fish, I suppose, because after a half-century of conditioning I find it too hard a habit to break. Put me on ethical-eating trial—challenge me to justify my decision—and you can expect stammering, stuttering, apology, and occasional weak attempts at self-justification. Clearly, my middle initial, W., does not stand for willpower.

But this is not about the decision to eat meat. It is about the exotic.

Until recently, "exotic" simply meant that something—a food, an animal, a shrub—came from another country. Once trade routes were opened, wealthy Europeans could not get enough of the interesting other, whether that meant a taxidermy giraffe or a live Tupinambá Indian marched into the French court to represent "the noble savage." The plains zebra is exotic in Scotland, in other words, but not in Zimbabwe. If eating the exotic is a sin against nature, then you are as guilty when you put a banana on your granola as I was eating zebra just after downing that Scottish pint.

All of this, of course, is such a fortunate dilemma for our species.

Dietary choices used to be simple: we ate what was given us by geography. If we lived in the far, frigid north, we learned to savor seal meat. If we lived in Montana, there were bison running by the thousands over the plains. The Norwegians hunted reindeer. We needed protein to live another day, and so we ate the protein that was available.

Now we can overnight live lobsters from Maine, fresh shrimp from the Gulf, free-range grass-fed beef from Argentina. We might heighten the interest with a little French Gruyère, perhaps accompanied by a rare Willamette Valley pinot noir.

We eat like kings, and like kings, we are often tempted to colonize the planet.

There are clearly downsides, dangers, and excesses to be found in this new world dinner order, but it is not as simple as just going back to the way it was, at least not for those of us living in urban America. If we were to simply eat what protein is available, we would have to quickly grow fond of alley cat and pigeon.

Those polar bears I mentioned in my opening, the ones who waited for the frozen mackerel I would toss across the moat, tried more than once to kill me. When I approached their enclosure from the back end, where the public didn't go, there was a steel door, and behind the steel door were bars. When I would go around to hose down the concrete "den" these polar bears retreated to when the heat or the crowds became too much for them, I would open that steel door and then quickly jump back three paces, because more often than not, within a split second, a massive yellow-white paw would slip around from the side, from where the polar bear was hiding, just out of view.

The regular zookeeper, Gus, a gruff German immigrant ticking off his days to retirement, schooled me on this. "Just 'cause you don't see him, 'cause you think he's outside or something, don't mean he didn't hear you come in and isn't waitin' to snag you." Gus would pause here, for effect, and then add: "He probably can't pull you through those bars, but do you wanta find out?"

The polar bear ate what was available. Whatever he could get his hands on, so to speak.

If a polar bear had been drinking in the Thistle Street Bar in Edinburgh with me that evening, I'm pretty sure he would have been up for a zebra burger, just as I was. He would have worried about it a bit less, probably, and would likely have ordered a water buffalo burger as well.

Afterward, chances are, the two of us would have stumbled out onto Queen Street, maybe had another pint or two, shared a few laughs.

And then, I feel fairly certain, he would have eaten me.

A Question from
BARRIE JEAN BORICH

Mister Essay Writer Guy

Dear Mister Essay Writer Guy:

I've recently discovered the satellite feature of Google Maps, and while zooming in on my own address, I found I'm able to see into my neighbors' apartments. Most of the blinds are closed, but I can make out the shapes of women and men in all combinations cooking, getting dressed, watching television, kissing, and playing the Xbox game that teaches people how to dance. I want to write the Great American Essay about all these folks, their dinner parties and affairs and fights and dance talents, but all I can see through the blinds are shadows. What are the ethics of writing about people who don't know I'm looking in their windows? And it's okay to invent stuff about my neighbors' lives to make a better story, right?

Sincerely,

Barrie Jean Borich
Chicago, Illinois

Dear Barrie,

Or is it Barrie Jean? I've been meaning to ask which is the best way to address you, but I've also been meaning to lose fifty pounds, and you can see just how poorly that has gone. When I say "you can see," I am hoping you turn to my author photo and that you can't *actually*, through a Google Earth search, see me waddling around in boxer shorts.

In any case, I love Google Maps, because they allow me to waste so much time on my computer, staring at places I'll never go, rather than writing that Great American Essay you talk about.

Merrily we surf away,

Mister Essay Writer Guy

P.S. Those looking for a digital version of the essay that follows can hop on over to tinyurl.com/plimptonmap. Unless the imminent polar bear apocalypse destroys the Internet, in which case, you're entirely on your own.

Mr. Plimpton's Revenge

A Google Maps Essay, in Which George Plimpton
Delivers My Belated and Well-Deserved Comeuppance

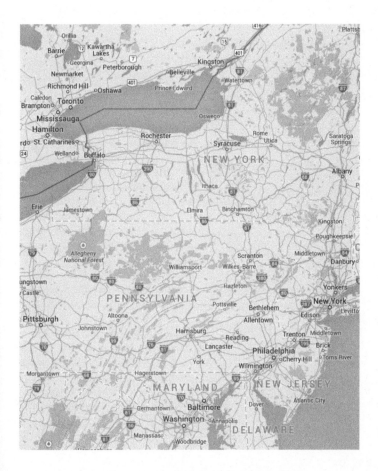

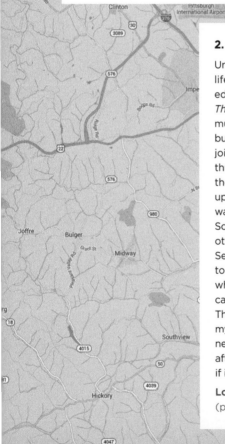

1. Or perhaps because I had a car . . . ?

When esteemed author and editor George Plimpton was invited to speak at the University of Pittsburgh in 1977, I was designated to chauffeur him around town, because I was thought to be among the most reliable of undergraduate writing majors.

Location: University of Pittsburgh

2. Well, semireliable . . .

Unfortunately, I lived a bit of a double life back then. By virtue of being editor of the campus newspaper, *The Pitt News*, I juggled and met multiple deadlines on a daily basis, but I was also lighting the proverbial joint from both ends. At midnight three nights a week, those of us on the newspaper staff would wrap up the next morning's paper and walk the page layouts to the printer. Some of us went home to sleep, a few others found cheap beer in one of the Semple Street bars, and I went directly to my friend Donny Rizzo's house, where we would smoke dope and play cards until five or six in the morning. Then I would go home, sleep through my classes, and show up again at the newspaper office around two in the afternoon. I stuck to this routine as if it were a religion.

Location: Donny Rizzo's House (precise address redacted)

3. I believe there was mescaline involved . . .

So the night before I was scheduled to retrieve Mr. Plimpton, I smoked a bit too much weed, which made me sleepy, until someone convinced me to take speed, which made me jittery, and then someone handed me two pills and said, "Hey, it's made from cactus! Cactus is healthy." This was a long time ago, and I don't endorse nor fully understand the choices I made back then, but the fact is that by nine in the morning, I was as high as the forty-second story of the University of Pittsburgh's towering Cathedral of Learning . . .

Location: Cathedral of Learning, University of Pittsburgh
4200 Fifth Avenue
Pittsburgh, PA 15213

4. A thoroughly gracious and entirely tall man

. . . yet there was nothing to do but head to the airport in my banged-up Datsun, a $400 clunker with clay fenders and a missing back window. Mr. Plimpton, one of the pioneers of what was then called New Journalism, believed that writers needed to immerse themselves in the subject matter rather than remain passive observers, so he had sparred with light heavyweight champion Archie Moore, had ridden the high trapeze for the Ringling Brothers and Barnum & Bailey Circus, had pitched in Yankee Stadium, and for his most celebrated book, *The Paper Lion*, had participated in scrimmages during the Detroit Lions' preseason training. So I imagine my rickety-clickety little car didn't frighten him much.

I remember that he was thoroughly gracious.

And tall. Very tall.

Location: Pittsburgh International Airport

5. The Parkway

As is so often the case when one picks up a famous writer, I didn't know what to say, but I couldn't stop talking.

Location: Fort Pitt Bridge

6. Kung pao chicken with extra stupid

Mr. Plimpton, it turned out, was hungry after his flight, so when we rolled near campus around noon, we stopped at a Chinese restaurant on Forbes. My memory is of trying very hard to communicate, yet finding that my words, and questions, confused even me. Too many drugs, not enough sleep.

Mr. Plimpton ate quickly. I may have eaten as well, or perhaps I just prattled on while stuffing egg rolls into my shirt pocket. In the end, Mr. Plimpton had to pay for lunch because my last five dollars had gone into the gas tank. It was not my best day.

Location: 3602 Forbes Avenue
Pittsburgh, PA 15213

7. Intelligent, erudite, and wry . . .

But eventually, I delivered Mr. Plimpton safely to his hotel. I slept a bit and then went to his talk that night. He was his usual intelligent, erudite, wry self.

This was thirty-two years ago.

Location: Webster Hall
101 N. Dithridge Street
Pittsburgh, PA 15213

8. Looming crisis

And the story would end right there, and it should have, honestly, except I was editor of the *Pitt News*, as I've explained, and one of those endless state budget crises was looming, education funding was about to be slashed, and the chancellor of the university had decided to send four student leaders to Harrisburg to speak to the legislature. He also sent one boy reporter—that would be me.

Location: Pennsylvania State Capitol House
2-228 Capitol Complex
Harrisburg, PA 17101

9. "I'm not sure you remember me, Mr. Plimpton . . ."

Waiting to fly home from the hearings that evening, sitting in the minuscule Harrisburg airport, minding my own damn business, I looked up, and just across the way, maybe eight feet from where I sat devouring a jelly donut, sat George Plimpton, the author, reading a book. I'm not clear what he was doing in the Harrisburg airport, but it is a fair guess that he was on an endless loop of visiting writer gigs. Making money as a writer is difficult, and it has long been known that Mr. Plimpton bankrolled the *Paris Review* out of his own pocket. Mr. Plimpton looked up. I caught his eye. He smiled weakly. I went over and shook his hand. "I'm not entirely sure if you remember me, Mr. Plimpton, but I was your escort . . ."

He remembered. I could see it in his eyes. But true to the man, he thanked me graciously, and I backed off.

It can be fairly surmised that Mr. Plimpton was not anxious to resume our conversation, whatever it may have been about.

Location: Harrisburg International Airport
1 Terminal Drive
Middletown, PA 17057

10. "Jake—it's Chinatown"

Which would, again, be the end of the story, except four weeks later I graduated from the university, and my friends and I—these were the dope fiend friends, not the student journalists—decided to visit New York City to celebrate. We dropped acid in Chinatown and rode the elevator to the top of the World Trade Center. But that's another story . . .

Location: Chinatown
New York, NY

11. Herkman could fondle a cymbal for hours . . .

The next morning we went to Manny's Music Store, near Times Square, because my friend Herkman wanted to fondle the newest Zildjian cymbals. Some sort of spiritual connection ensued, and we were in the back of the store forever, because after all, Herkman was a drummer, and obsessed (and probably still a little high). I had very little interest in cymbals or, by that point, Herkman, so I tottered out onto 48th Street, leaned against the storefront, and was entirely surprised to see—yes, of course—Mr. Plimpton, exiting a small door directly across the street, a stack of manuscripts in his arms.

Location: Manny's Music
156 W. 48th Street
New York, NY 10036

12. The word *stalker* was not much in use in those days . . .

Plimpton crossed the street directly toward me, his mind clearly elsewhere. He wore a crisp blue blazer and Harvard tie. "Hey," I called. "Mr. Plimpton . . ."

The Paper Lion looked up, his eyes widened, and he did a classic double take before faking right, then left, then speeding off toward Seventh Avenue on foot. Who could blame him? Surely Plimpton hadn't expected to see me again so soon. If ever.

Location: Manny's Music
156 W. 48th Street
New York, NY 10036

13. By an act of grace

Which would—again—be the absolute end of this story, except that twenty-six years later, I am by some act of grace a writer, with books of my own, two of them vaguely Plimptonesque (participatory, nonfiction), and I find myself on the faculty of a national nonfiction conference outside of Baltimore. The keynote speaker is, inevitably, George Plimpton.

Location: Goucher College
1021 Dulaney Valley Road
Towson, MD 21286

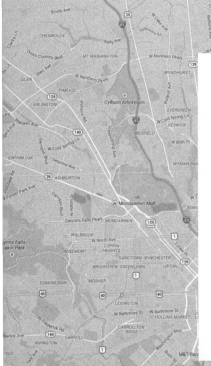

14. An ominous encounter . . .

In an odd way, I connect our decades-earlier meeting to my decision to write literary nonfiction. There is no logical method to explain this, given that our Chinese restaurant discussion is lost to the winds, and probably made no sense, but somehow it seemed that fate had been giving me a poke, a message, a hint, back then. Why did we keep meeting up? At a time in my life that I was the most lost?

This makes no sense. The most important turns in life, in some odd way, usually don't.

Location: Goucher College
1021 Dulaney Valley Rd.
Towson, MD 21286

15. And then, my comeuppance

All these many years later, Plimpton is still tall, still gracious. Still erudite and wry. At Goucher College that evening, he is brilliant and wise, and humble, and then signs dozens upon dozens of books. I hover near the signing table, trying to decide whether or not to bring our unfortunate past association to his attention, or to leave embarrassing enough alone. Earlier, I had shared my story with two of my fellow faculty members, hamming it up a bit for laughs, but telling all of this to Mr. Plimpton himself seemed potentially awkward. Or cruel?

The final book signed, the last hand shook, and he stands up from the table, walks in a direct line toward me. I look up.

Plimpton is smiling. "I remember you," he says. "You drove me from the airport."

I am dumbfounded, twitter-pated, thunderstruck. He holds his eyes steadily on mine, awaits my response.

At which point, one of my fellow faculty members appears at Plimpton's shoulder, her grin far too wide, giving the practical joke away.

She had told him.

He agreed to lead me on.

A tall, wry, erudite, gracious, and very funny man.

Location: Goucher College
1021 Dulaney Valley Road
Towson, MD 21286

A Question from
LIA PURPURA

Mister Essay Writer Guy

Dear Mister Essay Writer Guy,

I found this fragment in my journal: ". . . what's most urgent today is making sense . . ." Did you write that? I think you did. But can you elaborate? Making sense of . . . what exactly? As opposed to . . . not making sense? Why would someone want to do THAT?

Thanks,

Lia Purpura
Baltimore, Maryland

Dear Lia,

I just spent a good five minutes trying to make sense of your question, after which I took a good shower, toweled off, and had a two-hour nap. Now I think I am ready to tackle my answer:

What?

Okay, so Joan Didion, one of the finest essayists ever to put neuroses to paper, once said: "I write to find out what I'm thinking, what I'm looking at, what I see, and what it means." Which leads us to ask, if Ms. Didion doesn't know what she thinks, or what it means, what hope is there for anyone else? Probably not much, so let me go in another direction.

We are essayists, and we try. We explore. We discover. We want to know about every little thing in the world.

We attempt, for instance, to understand the intricacies of the human brain.[1]

Yours, in futile sense making,[2]

Mister Essay Writer Guy

---

1. A note to the reader: I come from the school of nonfiction writers that holds to the truth, as best as it can be assembled, given the vagaries of memory. The careful reader, however, might notice that I took a few liberties with truth in the essay that follows here, "Understanding Your Cauliflower." Think of this essay, then, in the tradition of our finest humorists and exaggerators—Twain, Benchley, Thurber, or any recent House or Senate candidates.

2. I feel confident, by the way, that you, dear reader, would have been able to sort that out without the preceding little footnote, but it is the other reader, the one across the bookstore from you, whom I most worry about.

Understanding Your Cauliflower

Let us begin with a logic challenge:

Miranda's mother had four children.

The first child was named April.

The second, May.

The third, June.

Now, what is the name of the fourth child?

Try briefly to make some sense of that while I tell you how the brain works:

The brain is like a cauliflower:

1. It is ugly.

2. It is about the size of a cauliflower.

Now that you know most of what there is to know about the brain, here's the solution to the puzzle:

Miranda's mother's fourth child was named Miranda.[1]

Okay. Let me throw another brainteaser your way. Try your very best to make sense of this one:

A man needs to cross a river in a canoe. With him, he has a bag of grain, a chicken, and a fox. He can carry only one of the three

---

[1]. If, by odd chance, you named the semi-well-known actress and movie director Miranda July, you can take half credit.

at a time. If he leaves the grain and the chicken behind on the riverbank, the chicken will eat the grain. If he takes the grain, the fox will eat the chicken. How does he successfully cross the river with his load?

While you are pondering that copious mystery, here's some further information on the brain, because science is sometimes just so freaking amazing:

- The brain can be divided into three basic units: the forebrain, the midbrain, and the hindbrain. The hindbrain includes the upper part of the spinal cord, the brain stem, and a wrinkled, repulsive ball of tissue called the cerebellum.
- The cerebellum coordinates blinking and nodding off.
- The rest of the hindbrain is used mainly for fantasizing about people's backsides. For instance, if you are walking down the street, and a fetchingly attractive person in tight denim jeans walks by, and your eye is pulled in by the bobbing motion of the hind-cheeks, you are using your hindbrain.
- The hindbrain looks like a cantaloupe. It is rounded. And orange on the inside.

Okay, now let me solve the puzzle of the man who needed to cross the river:

Foxes are actually pretty good swimmers. If you have a fox, let it go. If it loves you, it will swim across the river to find you. If not, the fox was never really yours.

Here, now try this one:

> One day two pieces of cauliflower, who were the very best of
> friends, were walking together down the street. They stepped
> off the curb and a speeding car came careening around the
> corner and ran one of them over. The uninjured cauliflower
> called 911 and helped his injured friend as best he was able.
> The injured cauliflower was taken to the emergency room and
> rushed into surgery. After a long and agonizing wait, the doctor
> finally appeared. He told the uninjured cauliflower, "I have
> good news, and I have bad news. The good news is that your
> friend is going to pull through."

Here's the puzzle: what was the bad news?

Think about that while we learn even more about our magical
human thinking organ:

- Your cauliflower-like brain is divided not just into three basic
  cantaloupe-shaped sections, but also into lobes. Neurosurgeons
  may or may not call them canta-lobes.

- To understand each lobe and its specialty, one must take a tour
  of the cerebral hemispheres, though a warning is in order here—
  these tours are quite popular, and you should try to book months
  in advance. (You can get wonderful bargains in the off-season!)

- The tour starts with the two frontal lobes, which lie directly
  behind the forehead. The lobes are shaped like little loaves of rye
  bread, and pair quite well with a dollop of dandelion jam. These
  frontal lobes act as short-term storage sites. If you are heading
  to the basement to grab a screwdriver, for instance, and want to
  remember once you reach the bottom step what it is that took

you down into the dark musty basement in the first place, you will use your frontal lobe.

- You can also store bits of string or acorns in the frontal lobes. Or, for that matter, a small screwdriver, and then you can skip going down into the basement altogether.

- Behind the frontal lobes, then, are the parietal lobes. Medical experts have yet to determine what these lobes do, though one poor soul who had them removed did the chicken dance for ten straight years, stopping only to sleep and to send envelopes filled with white powder to members of the city council.

- There are also occipital lobes, which process images from the eyes and link that information with images stored in your memory. You really shouldn't be looking at pornography, though, so let's just move on.

- The last lobes on our tour of the cerebral hemispheres are the temporal lobes, which lie in front of the visual areas and nest under the parietal and frontal lobes. At the top of each temporal lobe is an area responsible for receiving information from the ears.

- For instance, right now my ears are trying to tell me, "We stick out too much. And we are filled with wax."

What are *your* ears trying to tell *you*? Isn't it time that you listened?

So that's the brain. Everything that scientists have determined up to this point. You are now essentially qualified to become a brain surgeon. And to think, there are people who say they are too busy to read books!

Now here's the answer to the final puzzle:

> The doctor said of the injured cauliflower, "I have good news, and I have bad news. The good news is that your friend is going to pull through."

What was the bad news?

> "The bad news is that he's going to be a vegetable for the rest of his life."

A Question from
SUE WILLIAM SILVERMAN

Mister Essay Writer Guy

Dear Mister Essay Writer Guy,

On the face of it, I don't suppose there's a direct connection, per se, between being a cannibal and an essay writer. However, I have a first-semester student who is desirous, even insistent, about using imagery and metaphor that constantly refer to cannibalism. Is this okay? Might I even support her by acknowledging a connection between cannibalism and writing about dark family secrets? Could one argue, for example, that we cannibalize our families once we start rooting around and incorporating their dark, damp stories into our own? When we write about the less-than-wholesome attributes of those close to us, are we in fact (as this student claims) practicing a kind of devouring love? The student freely admits that Jeffrey Dahmer is a literary influence, even insisting that he inspired her to be a brutally honest writer—"Don't let anything, legal or illegal, stand in your way—and let the bone splinters fall where they may." What do you suggest? Should I humor her or steer her toward a more savory trope?

Sincerely confused,

Sue William Silverman
Grand Haven, Michigan

Dear Sue,

Thanks so much for that question. There is nothing quite like the memory of Jeffrey Dahmer and the concept of folks devouring human flesh to add extra funny when one is attempting to write a humorous book.

I owe you one,

Mister Essay Writer Guy

How Tasty Was
My Little Frenchman

In August of 1563, Michel de Montaigne, the father of the essay form, was in Rouen, France, at the invitation of King Charles the Ninth. It is not entirely clear why King Charles invited Montaigne, since the French monarch was only thirteen years old at the time and Montaigne doesn't come immediately to mind as a rollicking playtime companion.

Perhaps the young king needed Montaigne's help with his high school admissions essay?

In any case, also at Rouen that fateful weekend were three Tupinambá Indians, natives of what we now call Brazil, who had been lured onto a ship and transported to Europe for reasons not fully established by the historical record. One theory (mine) is that the French wanted these fellows to taste the *coq au vin*.

But it gets even more interesting: these men were cannibals. Thus it is entirely likely that if they *had* tasted the *coq au vin* and enjoyed its many aromatic satisfactions, and if they *had* taken the recipe back to the rain forest on small index cards, they would have eventually applied their newly gained culinary knowledge to meats other than the thigh of the chicken.

But everything is better with pearl onions and a red wine reduction, *non*?

Oui!

Montaigne was impressed by the flesh-eating Brazilian natives, or so he suggests in his essay "Of Cannibals."[1] In conversation with the trio of anthropophagus gentlemen, aided by "so ill an interpreter, and one who was so perplexed by his own ignorance to apprehend my meaning, that I could get nothing out of him of any moment," Montaigne was somehow still able to establish that the Brazilian natives:

(a) were flabbergasted to see "so many tall men, wearing beards, strong, and well-armed" bowing down to a thirteen-year-old child, and

(b) were equally perplexed as to why the starving, emaciated Frenchmen seen begging just outside the doorways of the puffy and prosperous upper classes "did not take the others by the throats, or set fire to their houses."

The cannibals do seem fairly reasonable (and in fact, on that latter point, somewhat prescient[2]), if we care to trust the oblivious interpreter.

---

1. The translation relied upon here is: Montaigne, Michel de. "Of cannibals." Trans. Charles Cotton. 1580. *Quotidiana*. Ed. Patrick Madden. 26 Dec 2006. http://essays.quotidiana.org/montaigne/cannibals. Among other notable details in Montaigne's essay, we learn that the Tupinambá wives apparently "employ to promote their husbands' desires, and to procure them many spouses; for being above all things solicitous of their husbands' honour, 'tis their chiefest care to seek out, and to bring in the most companions they can, forasmuch as it is a testimony of the husband's virtue." We have a name for this sort of solicitous procurement in the modern world, but it would perhaps not be polite to name it here.

2. Do you find the French revolting? Well, you might have if you'd visited in 1789.

These visitors from afar apparently offered additional sage reflection that day, but, Montaigne writes, when asked "what of all the things they had seen, they found most to be admired," they had three answers, "of which I have forgotten the third, and am troubled at it . . ."

The father of the essay, it seems, lacked a simple notebook and pencil. This, as a matter of fact, is why we now have university degrees focused on the writing of nonfiction, so that such catastrophic oversights never occur again.

In any case, and I am just speculating here, perhaps the third thing the flesh-eating dignitaries said that day was, "Monsieur de Montaigne, why is it exactly that your essays—which we digested with great interest on our long ocean voyage—rely so heavily on short snippets of wisdom culled from Cicero, Horace, Plutarch, and Virgil? Can you not rely upon your own individual thoughts and observations to make a point, without devouring every mental nugget these philosophers left behind? Exactly which of us is the cannibal in the room?"

Now those exact words may have been hard to articulate in the native Tupinambá language—I confess to having let my Tupinambá translation skills slide a bit since my college days—but the three gentlemen in question also had use of gestures, snorting noises, and skeptical raisings of the eyebrows, so I feel confident the point could have been made, had they urgently wished to do so.

I don't know, of course, if any of this makes sense. I am doubtful.

We are cannibals, those of us who write the Montaignean essay. We are cannibals as well, those of us who chop and grind our family memories to write memoir. Poets and fiction writers are not so much different.

Or playwrights, for that matter.

Or painters.

We take what we see, hear, smell, taste, and touch, and everything we have read, heard, or think that we remember having read or heard, and process it into the hunk of meat that forms the basis of our literary *coq au vin*.

And then sometimes it goes too far.

Did you know that Diego Rivera, the celebrated Mexican painter, claimed to have consumed human flesh at least three times, out of curiosity, feasting on fresh cadavers purchased from the city morgue?

Yes. He was proud of this.

Frida Kahlo, later in her life, when both her love for Diego and her health were in sharp decline, wrote a love poem to Rivera in which she referred to him as "the useless toad" good only for eating "in tomato sauce."

With pearl onions and a red wine reduction, who knows?

Only the Tupinambá Indians, and they aren't much around these days.

A Question from
B. J. HOLLARS

Mister Essay Writer Guy

Dear Mister Essay Writer Guy,

I recently found myself on the receiving end of a practical joke. (Though the joke, in my opinion, was hardly practical given the cost and logistics of renting so many barnyard animals for little more than a feces-gathering initiative.) I won't get into specifics, except to note that given the large quantity of laxatives that donkey must have consumed, I felt it my moral obligation to contact the American Society for the Prevention of Cruelty to Animals. Suffice it to say, mistakes were made, my Nikes are ruined, and I still have little to no understanding of what dung beetles find so terribly appealing about dung.

All of this leads me to my question: how is a serious-minded writer such as myself to craft an essay on such a thoroughly humiliating experience?

With great admiration,

B. J. Hollars
Eau Claire, Wisconsin

Dear B. J.,

You live in a town whose name sounds suspiciously like a cream-filled donut, and you are asking me to discuss humiliation?

And then there is your name.

C'mon B. J., don't make me go there!

My own humiliation essay follows. I just hope I don't embarrass myself.

Admonishingly,

Mister Essay Writer Guy

"Have You Learned Your Lesson, *Amigo*?"

Strolling up Madrid's Paseo de Recoletos one stifling July evening, my wife and I are accosted by a tall, worried-looking Spaniard. "Do you know where I find Calle de Serrano?" he asks.

The man gestures broadly, his movements quick and impatient. Clearly, he is late for an appointment. I guess him to be about forty-five years old—close to my age at the time. He wears a cheap linen sports coat, old trousers, and speaks comprehensible, but thickly accented, English. He needs a haircut.

Calle de Serrano is just one long block over from the wide *paseo* on which my wife and I have taken our evening walk, and I am about to explain this when a fourth figure dissects our triad. This time it is a small man, in a navy blazer and khaki pants, with dark eyes and hair and a distinct air of authority. He is probably in his mid-fifties. "Do you know this man?" he asks me.

"No." I shake my head.

The small man nods, flashes a badge in a dark leather wallet. He allows a second or two until my face registers that I have seen the insignia, and then pockets the badge and turns to the taller man. "Let me see your passport," he demands, his voice firm.

The man who needed directions, or at least pretended to need directions, begins to fumble in his various pockets.

"You have to be careful," the police officer warns, keeping his eyes on the tall man. "Careful of strangers."

I nod again.

"Your passport," the policeman repeats sharply.

The tall man makes a face. He is clearly disgusted.

As a stranger in Madrid, I can only imagine the source of his disgust. I don't understand the ethnic and class divisions of this city—or of Spain—nearly well enough to discern what is happening here. I have been warned about Moroccans, the supposed thieves of Madrid, and it occurs to me that the tall man might be Moroccan. I am eyeing him suspiciously.

At the same time, I am aware that he may be disgusted exactly for this reason: that perhaps he has been singled out for his ethnicity, or his class, or the way that he dresses. An innocent man, looking for directions, tired of living under a constant cloud of mistrust. Back home, we call it racial profiling.

Or possibly he is disgusted because he is guilty and has just been caught. Maybe this man is arrested every three nights or so and is dismayed by the prospect of once more going to jail, posting bail, facing a hearing—all the rigmarole that defines the life of a recidivist criminal in the United States justice system.

Eventually, after checking numerous pockets, the tall man produces a worn passport, suggesting, I suppose, that he is indeed a foreigner in Madrid.

The police officer scrutinizes the document closely, though it is difficult for any of us to see very much—the hot Madrid sun has set, and we are in the dark shadows of a lush line of trees along the *paseo*. In fact, we are but a few yards from the Café Gijón, long famed as a gathering place for artists, intellectuals, and bullfight aficionados. Hemingway had been to Gijon a few times, referring to the scholarly clientele as "windbags."

The officer returns the passport and gestures with his hand that the man should remain in place. Then he turns to me. "May I see yours as well, sir?" he asks.

I produce a photocopy of my passport, from my neck wallet.

"An American," he says with a smile.

At this moment, I am grateful and relieved. I am in Madrid teaching a month-long class, and one of my students, Katie, just the week before had lost her wallet, her camera, and her passport to a pair of strangers in a café—one, an old woman, who feigned interest in Katie's infant child, and a second, unseen, who used the planned distraction to lift her purse. On this end of town, at least, the Madrid police are clamping down. It is surprising how much can go through your mind in a few seconds, because in addition to all of this, I am also feeling a bit sheepish again, a bit of American guilt. This is the Salamanca neighborhood, a prosperous end of the city, and thus it is protected. My student and her husband and child stayed in a less posh neighborhood and fell victim. Class is everywhere.

The plainclothes detective checks my wife's passport as well, and the tall man, still impatiently shifting on his feet, asks, "Can I go?"

"No, no," the policeman warns. "Let me see your money."

Due perhaps to the sharp tone and clear authority, the tall man does not hesitate. He opens his wallet to show a few crumpled twenty-euro notes. The police officer holds them up to the dim streetlight.

"Counterfeiting," he explains to me politely. "We have a lot of counterfeit money around this summer."

He returns the tall man's cash and asks, then, to see mine. "You have to be careful that no one gives you the counterfeit bills."

I am tempted to explain that no money has changed hands between the lanky Moroccan and me and thus there is no reason to check, but I decide against it. It is simpler to let the man do his job. Besides, though we are all speaking English, I am not sure how well I am understood.

I open my wallet, show the man that I have 200 euros and a Visa card.

"Put the card away," he says. "Put that back in your wallet."

Of course, how stupid of me, flashing my wealth around. But I feel safe. The police are right here.

"Can I go?" the tall man asks again. If he was late before, he is very late now.

There is a sharp exchange, the first moment when I actually sense anger, or danger. Harsh words are traded in Spanish. My language skills are paltry, but the body language is clear: the tall man shouldn't even think about going anywhere and should stop asking.

The police officer hands me back my money, folded exactly as I handed it to him less than a minute earlier. "Now put that away, quickly," he warns.

I comply.

"You can't be too careful," he offers in a calmer, reassuring tone. He looks from my wife to me and smiles again. "It is best not to speak to strangers on the street." He gestures to the west. "Especially on the Gran Via."

"*Sí*," I say. I don't know why I switch to Spanish here. Most likely, I want the man to like me.

"Can I go now?" the Moroccan asks once more.

"Yes." The officer waves him off with no apology.

The man shrugs, looks deeply insulted. He mumbles, "I was only asking for directions," and is gone.

The policeman reaches out to shake my hand. "Thank you, sir," he says. "I appreciate your patience." He points to my camera and smiles. "Very expensive?"

"No, not so much," I say.

He smiles even more broadly.

I shake his hand. "*Gracias*." I express my appreciation with a Spaniard's pronunciation and feel good about that.

I like this city more and more, especially now that I have been reassured the Madrid police are out on the tourist walkways, unseen and stealthy, guarding us from all sorts of thieves and scammers.

But, of course, here is what really happened:

> *Strolling up Madrid's Paseo de Recoletos one stifling July evening, my wife and I are accosted by a tall, worried-looking Spaniard. "Do you know where I find Calle de Serrano?" he asks.*

This all occurred, exactly as described.

> *We are interrupted by a small man in a navy blazer and khaki pants. He is probably in his midfifties. "You have to be careful," the police officer warns, keeping his eyes on the tall man. "Careful of strangers."*

How did he know to speak English?

> *The tall man makes a face. He is clearly disgusted. I have been warned about Moroccans, the supposed thieves of Madrid, and it occurs to me that the tall man might be Moroccan.*

And of course, both of these men know that.

> *The police officer scrutinizes the man's passport closely, though it is difficult for any of us to see much—we are in the dark shadows of a lush line of trees along the* paseo.

Later, much later, it occurs to me that the police officer would have been insane—certainly unprofessional, and perhaps negligent—not to move us under a streetlight, or closer to the illumination and safety of the outdoor cafe. A small knife can inflict great harm in just a second's time. That summer there is a story going around Madrid about a Greek tourist being knifed for her wallet in the Plaza Mayor. But the policeman seemed so sure of himself.

The officer returns the man's passport and gestures with his hand that the man should remain in place. Then he turns to me. "May I see yours as well, sir?" he asks.

He is gaining my trust. He asks of me exactly what he asks of the suspect—no more, no less. He is even-handed, democratic. This man understands Americans and our sense of political correctness better, apparently, than I understand the world of the *Madrileño.*

He asks, then, to see my money. I am about to explain that no money has changed hands between the lanky Moroccan and me and thus there is no reason to check, but I do not. It is simpler to let the man do his job. Besides, though we are all speaking English, I am not sure how well I am understood.

I have begun to think of the tall man as Moroccan, though I have no proof, just my adopted prejudice. Maybe they counted on that too? Why else did they plant a passport on the taller man? I am disoriented many times over—an American traveling in Spain, unsure of the customs, unsure of the language, unsure, even, of what sort of man I am dealing with. They know, of course, that Americans so often see crime through a lens of race and ethnicity.

"Can I go?" The tall man asks again. There is a sharp exchange, the first moment where I actually sense anger, or danger. Harsh words are exchanged in Spanish.

The sharp anger inevitably draws my eyes away from the police officer's hands, hands that at that second were holding my euro notes up to the dim light. My eyes, as well as my wife's eyes, dart to the face of the tall man, to the abrupt change in mood, the heightened tension, the possible excitement of police business. Americans watch too many police crime shows.

> *The officer hands me back my money, folded exactly as I handed it to him. "Now put that away, quickly," he warns.*

Because only a fool flashes his money on the street.

***

It is not necessary, I suppose, to explain that though the small, dark-eyed man did return my carefully folded money, he did not return all of it. He kept ninety euros, a sum he no doubt shared with the tall, disgusted fellow who I'm now sure was his partner in this skillful swindle. The badge? It looked real enough, but it was the man's clear sense of authority that fooled me more than the badge in the leather case.

A few details should have tipped me off—why was the entire exchange in English, for instance, even the majority of what passed between the pseudo-cop and the "Moroccan" suspect? If the smaller man suspected the tall man of thievery, why didn't he first ask me what had happened between us, instead of immediately demanding to see passports and wallets?

But it all occurred so quickly.

I feel a bit silly telling people this story, and stupid. Stupid that I fell for the dodge and silly for attempting now to make something more of it than what it seems clearly to have been: I was ripped off.

But the whole maneuver was brilliant in its way, starting with the careful gaining of my trust, followed by the flawless performance of the dismayed suspect, and capped off by the misdirection of my attention at the precise moment that something less than half of my money disappeared into the magician's hands. They might as well have strung me up like a puppet, I followed their directions so well.

Of course, I figured the scam out within five minutes, and counted the bills to confirm my suspicions. But had I been out for a night of drinking, or less certain of how much cash I had begun with that evening, I might never have known. Among the clever turns was that the men didn't take it all, didn't take too much, took just enough that it felt right slipping the notes back into my wallet. This unusual restraint was designed to ensure that I was not about to shout "Stop, thief!" and chase them down the boulevard. Even had I checked my wallet within thirty seconds of the parting handshake, both men had more than adequate time to slip away into the shadows.

I prefer to think of this event as street theater, though even as I type those words I can hear my friends snicker.

"You were ripped off, *hombre estupido*."

But I was in Madrid for five weeks, and my goal was to immerse myself in an unfamiliar culture, to experience something tangible, visceral, something outside of my normal experience. I wanted to escape the role of tourist-observer, and, as I said to my friends numerous times while planning the trip, to live "the day-to-day life" in someplace unknown, to feel "part of the place."

Excuse me for saying this, but as wonderful as it was to see firsthand the enormously impressive collection of art in the Museo del Prado—Bosch, El Greco, Titian—or Picasso's *Guernica* in the Centro de Arte Reina Sofia, and to witness the breathtaking architecture and ancient statuary of Madrid's central streets, what I am still fascinated by many years later is the artistry of the men who took my cash.

Like good theater, the event had a nuanced script. The men became the characters they were playing. Chances were taken. They nudged me, as superior actors will, to believe my role as well.

In any art form, I have always admired restraint, and they certainly had that.

But art is meant to enlighten. To offer lessons and provide insight into other lives and other worlds. Not to humiliate.

Well, though my snickering friends would be right in suggesting that this encounter was a tutorial on why I should never hand my money to strangers on the street, I prefer to think of another lesson learned. Something about being at the mercy of language and custom.

My inability to speak more than basic Spanish, my unfamiliarity with what was to be expected in this new culture and what was clearly out of the norm, my reluctance to assert my own self-interests because of fear of misunderstanding, all played a role.

Back home, my Filipino friend Andrea jokes about not understanding "white people." Though she speaks English better than I speak it, she carries with her a level of unease and confusion, and she feels at risk because of the way her American-born coworkers relate to one another in the corporate office. There are so many implied or invisible signals that we exchange, assumptions that we make, and she is pretty sure she gets a lot of them wrong.

If ever I should want to empathize more directly with Andrea, or with my foreign-born students, or with foreign strangers anywhere, the little street play entitled "You Think I'm a Cop, But I'm Not" has given me a way to understand.

Like all genuine art, it has opened my eyes.

***

Madrid is Hemingway's city, and Hemingway knew something about the inadequacy of fact. The truth he encountered as a journalist failed to satisfy his need for meaning, so he became a novelist, began to write of the world he wanted to see. Men of honor. Women who drank like men. Bulls who marched proudly into the ring, ready to die.

I can guess how Hemingway might have ended this story:

Later, on the Gran Via, the two men come up behind me with hearty back slaps and return the stolen money. "Have you learned your lesson, *amigo*?"

Or perhaps we all meet unexpectedly in a dusky Chueca tavern and exchange deep, knowing laughs. They buy the drinks.

But I am writing the truth. These two Spaniards ripped me off.

Splendidly.

A Question from
DIANE ACKERMAN

Mister Essay Writer Guy

Dear Mister Essay Writer Guy:

Why is there an "ess" in the essay?

Diane Ackerman
Ithaca, New York

Dear Diane,

Let me apologize right up front for where this is leading, but strictly speaking, there is no "ess" in the essay.

Instead, there is an "ass," since, of course, Montaigne used the French word *assaying* to describe what he was up to. *Assay,* meaning "to attempt."

So, if we were to be accurate, we'd have to ask, why is there an "ass" in the essay?

And then everyone would blush, grow uncomfortable, and wander out of the room.

Montaigne himself would not wander off, though, since he was fond of plain speaking. In "Of Experience," he recalls the storyteller Aesop, who, depending on your chosen translation, saw his master either "make water" or "piss" while walking, and said in response, "What then, must we dung as we run?"

So now look where your question has led us.

I have to go,

Mister Essay Writer Guy

Of Bums

1. Montaigne was a bum, of sorts. Well, not so much that any remaining Brooklyn Dodger fans might holler "Throw the bum out!" To be honest, Montaigne didn't even own a baseball glove, as best we can determine. He wasn't that sort of bum.

2. Another definition of bum is a vagrant, a hobo, or a tramp. I know something about hobos. Two blocks up from my childhood home, along 12th Street, ran some railroad tracks and a string of decrepit factories, and this hobo—somehow we knew his name was Andy—lived in an adjacent wooded area in a one-room plywood shack. Every once in a while, when bored, a group of us neighborhood boys would enter the small thicket of urban woods and throw rocks at Andy's thin walls. He would lurch out, wave his fist wildly, and chase us back to civilization. We were convinced that Andy wanted to catch and kill us, maybe violate us first, because he was a hobo, and that's what hobos did.

    Probably, in retrospect, he just wanted us to stop throwing rocks.

    Montaigne was not this kind of a bum—not homeless. Montaigne's father was given noble rank after fighting in Italy for King Francis I, and to commemorate his far-flung adventures, he built a castle decorated in the style of an ancient Roman villa. Montaigne inherited the castle. Not bad.

3. Bum can also mean one who does no work. Now Montaigne may have been this sort of a bum—depending on your definition of work. He spent a lot of time woolgathering, that's

for sure, and lots of us might classify that as a pure waste of time, unless you actually gathered the wool from sheep and made sweaters. But Montaigne didn't make sweaters, he made essays. The men I grew up with—machine operators, mechanics—had no use for that. They would have called the man a layabout, daydreamer, dillydallier, or slug.

At age thirty-seven, Montaigne retired. That may have raised a few eyebrows as well.

4. Bum—though it embarrasses me a bit to say so—also refers to the fleshy part of the human body that you are probably sitting on right at this moment. My yoga teacher likes to call them "butt-ox."

    Was Montaigne a buttock? Probably not.

    Did he have buttocks? Yes.

    Did he ever think about them? Surely.

    Here's what he said, in his essay "Of Experience":

    "Even on the highest throne in the world, we are still sitting on our ass."

5. Bum can be used as an adjective as well, as in bum luck or bum rap. I don't know if this one suits: Montaigne, it seems, had pretty good luck. A rich father. A castle. Special tutors and a household of servants instructed to speak to him only in Latin. Now I had none of that, but I'm not complaining.

Okay, I am.

But for all we know, Montaigne may have had a bum back.

For that, he should have met my yoga teacher.

6. And bum can be a verb—as in, may I bum a cigarette, may
   I bum a few quarters for the subway, or—in the case of
   Montaigne—may I bum an endless succession of Greek and
   Latin aphorisms to insert willy-nilly into my essays? Our
   French friend borrows extensively from Ovid, Virgil, Seneca,
   just about anyone who ever felt moved to jot down a few words
   in classical Greek or Latin. So this much we know: Montaigne
   was a grub, mooch, sponge.

   He was a bum. No doubt about it.

A Question from
DINAH LENNEY

Mister Essay Writer Guy

Dear Mister Essay Writer Guy,

Is there anything you won't write about? Anything too private?

(Would you admit it if there were?)

Dinah Lenney
Los Angeles, California

Dear Dinah,

May I tell you a story?

Ten years ago I attempted what I thought would be my third book of nonfiction, an autobiographical account of my relationship with my smart, independent, moody preteen daughter, and an attempt to wrestle with the issues raised by Mary Pipher in her important *Reviving Ophelia: Saving the Selves of Adolescent Girls*, a book that examines what Pipher calls our "girl-poisoning culture."

When I would tell people about this book, or read excerpts, I received universally positive reactions. "That's important, Dinty. Write it," folks would say at conferences. Even now, ten years later, people will still occasionally ask me, "Whatever happened to that book?"

Well, despite a nifty advance, the interest of two publishers, and the support of two excellent editors, the book eluded me, kept ringing false, wouldn't resolve itself in any satisfying way. I estimate that I wrote upward of 1,200 pages of material to complete the first "finished" draft of that book. I'm a constant reviser, so when I say "finished" draft, I'm talking twenty to thirty drafts, at a minimum, of each chapter. And yet it wasn't working, refused to take successful shape. The first publisher eventually lost interest.

Stubborn to the end, I embarked on a second attempt, a radical rethinking and reshaping of the book, and produced heaven only knows how many fresh pages, while entirely retooling what I recycled from the first iteration. A second publisher came on board. Briefly. Then lost interest too.

All in all, this project consumed five years.

***

One July afternoon, I sat in my literary agent's office, having driven into Manhattan just for the day, so we could discuss the next step with my stalled project. "Why don't you set it aside?" Carol suggested after some mutual hand-wringing. "Give the book a rest, and who knows, maybe you will come back to it in a few years. Let's see what else you have to work on."

I wanted to throttle Carol right then and there, and might have if I were not a believer in nonviolence (or if the receptionist had not been in such close hearing range). After all of this work, sweat, agony, she wanted me to set it aside, just like that?

I sputtered; she patted me down with consoling words; I sputtered some more and left her office in a state of suppressed rage, shock, despondency, and confusion.

Thirty minutes later, though, as I headed home across the George Washington Bridge, I felt as if the proverbial load had been lifted from my shoulders. Carol was exactly right. Despite the hard work, the soundness of my initial idea, the moments in the book that worked quite well (but not well enough to make the book complete or coherent), the project was making me unhappy, was likely to remain stalled for years to come, and my stubbornness to "finish what I had started" was sucking the life from my writing practice.

***

On the subject of writing about your own children, Alice Munro once said, "You can write about your parents when they're gone, but your children are still going to be here, and you're going to want them to come and visit you in the nursing home."

That's part of the problem, certainly. Whatever I wrote about my daughter, I had to live with, and so did she, and I didn't want to screw the relationship up any more than my ineptitude and the vicissitudes of her becoming a teenager already had.

Plus, I couldn't see clearly. Who can see clearly, when their own children are involved? And my particular kid? She was pretty adept at sending up smoke screens.

***

Not that those five years were wasted.

Eventually, I salvaged a four-page essay, which follows this letter, an essay that pretty much sums up everything I was trying to say in that book.

People tell me it is a good essay.

It oughta be. I calculate my final output amounts to one word every two days.

Wondering why anyone would choose to be a writer,

Mister Essay Writer Guy

Pulling Teeth, or Twenty Reasons Why My Daughter's Turning Twenty Can't Come Soon Enough

1. Here's an interesting fact: *homo erectus,* our 1.5-million-year-old evolutionary antecedent, skipped right over the teenage years, proceeding directly from cave kid to cave adult.

2. Researchers figured this out by taking cross-sections of fossilized teeth. Markings on tooth enamel, it seems, are much like tree rings. They tell us, for instance, that what modern human parents experience as an extended, oftentimes interminable period of adolescence developed only about a half million years ago.

3. Our ancestors were, in this way, like modern apes. Young apes break the apron strings much earlier than humans. By the time a female chimpanzee has reached her early teen years, she can make her own nest and locate her own bananas.

4. More important, if a day filled with grooming her simian cousins, gnawing on twigs, and swinging from branch to branch to attract boy chimps leaves a female teen chimp feeling somehow unfulfilled, she doesn't blame anyone but herself.

5. My point? Someone should yank the teeth out of every teenage boy in my daughter's high school classroom. (I have names, and addresses, if any scientists are interested.)

6. My other point? Those same scientists should pull a few girl molars as well, and put these female teeth under a microscope. My hope here is that these pioneering molarologists will discover that some invisible change is under way. After all, if teenagers can evolve once, they can surely evolve again. Perhaps evolve to where the prickly adolescent stage becomes just a vaporous memory.

7. I have a female teenager at home. The other day, I picked up a piece of paper on my desk. *My* desk. "Don't look at that!" my female teenager shouted. So I quickly returned the paper, and murmured, "Sorry, didn't know it was private." She huffed, "Of course it's private." What I seemed to be looking at, in the few short moments before I was bullied into putting it back down, was a line drawing of a young woman in a dress. I think the point of the artwork was the dress—an elaborate, original bit of *haute couture*. The design, understand, was drawn on *my* tablet, with *my* pencil. "How was I to know the drawing was private?" I asked, foolishly trying to remain in my daughter's good graces. My female teenager just glared at me, the way teenagers will glare when you have them dead to rights, when they know you're correct, and they hate you for it. "Listen," she said firmly. "From now on, just assume that *everything* I do is private."

8. I am not a perfect father. Instead, I'm pretty much the "hang in there" type. Meaning that I have almost no idea what I am doing, but over the years I've hung in there, plugging onward, trusting that instinct—or perhaps dumb luck—will get me through. Female teenagers, of course, naturally crave a level

of distance from their embarrassing, fragrant, loutish fathers, so lately I've given my daughter extra space—girls, after all, have the right to privacy. And there, then, is the rub: that space quickly begins to seem a distance, and that distance soon enough resembles a gulf. Before you know it, a gulf that neither party can step across.

9. Down this road are any number of horrible outcomes. I know. I've imagined them all.

10. I had the good fortune to take my female teenager to Madrid one summer. Now, admittedly, Madrid in July includes surly crowds, fearsome traffic, and scorching pavement, but still, come on, this was Europe. The capital of Spain. Museums, cafés, fashion. My female teenager just moped for most of the trip, primarily because her feet hurt and she didn't take at all well to Spanish cuisine. Or at least, that was my interpretation. "Why aren't you having fun?" I inquired. This is an absolutely brainless question to ask someone who seems not to be having fun, but I asked it nonetheless, more than once. "Jesus Christ," she answered. "Get over it." I persisted, stupidly imagining that I could somehow talk my daughter out of her bad humor. "You know," I said in a calm, parental voice, "it's hard for me to have a good time when I look over and you just seem so darned miserable." She chewed on my words a moment, gave them careful consideration, then spat back, "That's your problem."

11. That is my problem.

12. I wish someone had taken me to Europe when I was young.

13. That's my problem too.

14. But I don't know what she wants, or what I'm supposed to do, or how to remain a constructive influence while being systematically frozen out of every aspect of her teenage female life. Some days I want to pound the walls and just scream. How do you please someone who resents your very existence? How do you stop trying? Parents, especially embarrassing male parents, can be a drag sometimes, but they are a biological necessity, and as much as I'd like to apologize to my female teenager for the inconvenient reality of sperm and egg and family, it is not my fault. Not really. I'm not the one who came up with it.

15. Darwin had ten children, but interestingly, he didn't take any of them along to the islands.

16. So I'm back to evolution. Maybe, just maybe, evolution is occurring even now, and maybe female teenagers will soon enough develop beyond this tendency toward prickly unreasonableness. Perhaps this whole problem is just a half-million-year aberration, a necessary but ridiculous step along the evolutionary continuum.

17. Or possibly, like those Galapagos finches Darwin was so fond of, parents themselves will adapt new beaks, allowing them to more easily break open this tougher seed coating.

18. As for my daughter, she will stop being a teenager eventually. She will turn twenty. I've heard that can happen.

19. For now, though, just getting my female teenager to speak to me is like . . . well . . . like pulling teeth.

20. And I don't like pulling teeth. It tends to be painful on both ends.

A Question from
PHILIP GRAHAM

Mister Essay Writer Guy

Dear Mister Essay Writer Guy,

On those occasions when I wallow in the list of foolish things I've said or done in my life, my humiliation often leads me to the nearest multiplex, where I will watch the movie with the most elaborate car chases and heavily armed gun battles. This helps somewhat. Is this a good topic for an essay?

Signed,

Philip Graham
Urbana-Champaign, Illinois

Dear Philip,

Choosing topics *is* hard. Montaigne himself, the *père des pères* of the essay form, was raised reading the finest Greek and Roman orators, and he ended up writing about cannibals, thumbs, and whether or not the sweat exuded by Alexander the Great really stunk up the joint. Phillip Lopate, our contemporary master of the form, spends a fair amount of time in *Portrait of My Body* considering his penis, describing it at one point as "a pink mushroom."

So tread lightly my friend. Tread lightly,

Mister Essay Writer Guy

How to Choose an Appropriate Essay Topic

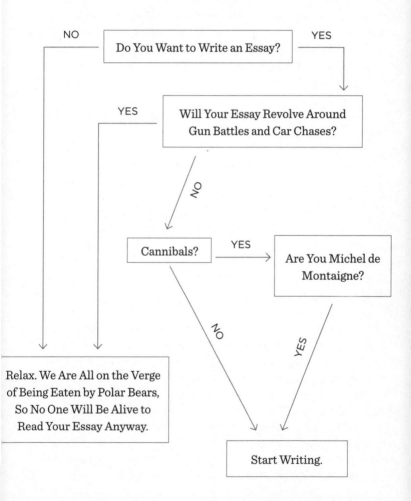

NO

Do You Want to Write an Essay?

YES

YES

Will Your Essay Revolve Around Gun Battles and Car Chases?

NO

Cannibals?

YES

Are You Michel de Montaigne?

NO

YES

Relax. We Are All on the Verge of Being Eaten by Polar Bears, So No One Will Be Alive to Read Your Essay Anyway.

Start Writing.

A Question from
MICHAEL MARTONE

Mister Essay Writer Guy

Dear Mister Essay Writer Guy,

Should I space once or twice after I have typed a period. I just spaced twice and used a period instead of a question mark to see what I would do. I did it again. Again. Still doing it. I will really try hard after this upcoming period not to space twice. Helpless. I feel this shows my age, as the kids today all seem to be spacing just once after a period. Here I actually spaced twice but deleted once. So my question is what's up with this, these typographical conventions that seem to be saying we should use our nifty modern high-powered type-setting machines like nineteenth-century typewriters? I spaced twice after the "?" too, or is it 2? I mean, do I have to draw you a picture about how I worry about wanting to use pictures in there with all my typing? It is so easy to do now. So I guess what I am asking is if I am writing essays, is it okay to worry about the ways the text I am typing looks? I mean, don't get me started about which font I should use. I spaced twice there. And there. That can keep me from writing for days. Please Mr. (should I space once or twice after that period?) Essay Writer Guy, what's up with the all these do's and don'ts of composing? By the way (or is it BTW or btw?) I am really getting into the ellipsis (. . .) but I don't know how many spaces between those periods . . . and when I do type an ellipsis (. . .) my machine (it is a Mac with Microsoft Word) corrects the spacing magically. Two spaces. Should I worry that the machine seems interested in the periods of the ellipsis (. . .) and not the other periods? Or am I just being spacey? HA! (Oh, God, I used an exclamation mark!)!

Michael Martone
Tuscaloosa, Alabama

Dear Michael,

What was your question? I'm sorry, I just spaced.

In any case, if the question had to do with writing, everything you need to know is in the following essay.

All best,

Mister Essay Writer Guy

Four Essential Tips for Telling the Truth in Memoir and Securing That Blockbuster Book Deal

With Helpful Writing Prompts and Exercises!!!

You want to be a writer, but you find yourself repeatedly stumped by the complex philosophical distinctions facing every beginning wordsmith—questions such as do you space once or twice after a period, and is there actually any difference between fact and fiction? Well, hey buster, who wouldn't be confused? Those spaces are tiny. And have you noticed that fact and fiction not only *both* begin with an "f," but they also share a "c" and a "t"?

It seems at times as if the universe is purposely trying to confuse us! Especially that "fact over fiction" one. Knowing the difference between what really happened to you a few years back and what you imagined only yesterday is a fantastically daunting challenge. I mean, are we expected to remain sober every moment of our lives?

There was, for instance, that worthless sap—James *Something*—who was sure that he had languished in a federal lockup for ten years or so, scarfing down baked ziti dinners with notorious Italian mobsters. He wrote that bestselling book about it. *A Million Little Pizzas*? Turns out, though, the guy spent only five hours in a small town Ohio police station.

Easy mistake. Could have happened to anyone.

But I digress. My goal is to present you with four essential tips to writing truthful memoir and securing that blockbuster book deal, and that's why you're here, right?

You want tips?

I got tips.

Four of them:

Telling the Truth in Personal Memoir Tip 1
Remember: It Is True Because You Wrote It

I wrote the following snippet when I was twenty-two years old. I remember writing it. Thus, it *is* memoir.

Be sure that you are sitting down when you read it:

> Occurrences are not alone and we are not apart from that which does occur if only when the stars are out and waters rise to lunar songs of times before they knew the moon was earth to men in solemn cubes of bluish light on evening rides with relatives and closer friends than even neighbors are

> Again

> The night it came when old men drank in musty bars and cherry bombed the bathrooms until laughter struck the night and whiskey breaths puffed home to lukewarm meals and upset women's hearts until morning drenched the sky and woke the men who panted off to work

> And times then came when women drove in drunken fear through whitened roads of shining hopes and banks of snowy fantasies until the metal touched and ripped and ran and wandered to a formal place where pistoled men write funny words and listen to their radios . . . so that they can drive you

home in emblemmed cars so neighbors can peek out and
wonder where the lady had gone wrong.

Jesus Christ, what was I thinking?

The truth is, I was high as a kite when I wrote those words. Stoned
solid.

I used a manual Royal typewriter because it made me feel more
like Hemingway. I eschewed almost all punctuation, because rules
are for suckers. Back then I lived alone in a shotgun apartment. My
best friend was the neighbor's shabby cat, Ajax.

Is "emblemmed" even a word?

> **Helpful Writing Prompt**
> Score some medical marijuana, regress to a fetus-like
> twenty-two years old, score an ancient typewriter on eBay,
> and connect with your pain.

Telling the Truth in Personal Memoir Tip 2
Remember: Fiction Has Its Own Sort of Truth

So here's the odd thing. Underneath my weed-induced crimes
against prose, just reproduced, there really was something that
I was trying to get at. Something about my father's severe
alcoholism—he was a stagger-home-every-night-drunk-at-
midnight-from-the-corner-tavern sort of drunk—and about my
mother's less obvious problems with drinking and depression. The
line from my juvenilia above "... *And times then came when women
drove in drunken fear through whitened roads of shining hopes and*

banks of snowy fantasies until the metal touched and ripped and ran . . ." refers to a real event, wherein my mom, way too soused to be behind the wheel, insisted on driving home anyway from a Christmas party with a young version of me in the backseat, only to sideswipe four cars on Eighth Street, during a near whiteout. The rest of that quasi-sentence—*"and wandered to a formal place where pistoled men write funny words and listen to their radios"*— refers to what happened next. Instead of stopping, or turning right onto Cranberry and slowly driving the two blocks that would take us home, my mom drove another two miles to City Hall, where she promptly turned herself in at the main police station.

True.

Weird.

Couldn't have made it up.

I wrote my emblematic "Howl," exploring and obfuscating my particular shame and agony, about eighteen years after the event, and then, another ten years later, when my ambition was no longer to become the new Allen Ginsberg but to become the new Raymond Carver, I wrote it again.

I changed the model of automobile, the name of the town, the details of the sideswipe, and my first name, and presented my childhood memory in a short story entitled "Just Tell Me What Happens Next":

> It is December, a week shy of Christmas . . . A snow flurry has moved into the Cumberland Valley, light but steady, and the road is visible only about twenty feet from the Corvair's front headlights.

My mother drives down a narrow street, soft flakes rushing past the edges of our car, as if we are driving through a tunnel. Heat pours from the car's dashboard, and I lean forward in my seat, trying to see where we are headed.

My mother gazes into the snow, gripping the steering wheel with both hands. No one else seems to be on the road, although once, as we round the corner onto Fourth Street, I hear the clank of tire chains.

The streetlights shine yellow, making the snow seem less than real. My mother slows down some after the Corvair hits an icy patch and fishtails.

"You okay?" I ask her.

"Don't worry, Russ honey. Your mom can drive."

"Where are we going?"

"I don't know."

I see Chambersburg's main intersection a half-block ahead, and though the car is only creeping at this point, I brace myself against the dash. My mother applies the brakes a few feet before the stop sign, but the road is slick, uncertain. Her small, red hands wrestle the steering wheel as we slide to a stop, a few feet beyond the sign.

"You okay, honey?"

I don't answer.

"It's just a little icy, baby. Just a little icy."

"We should go home," I say.

"A little icy."

My mother inches the Corvair through the snow again, trying to make the turn. "I'm a little tipsy," she tells me.

"Why don't we walk?"

"Mommy's just tipsy. It doesn't mean she can't drive."

So far so good, yes? Forward movement, characterization, the child's limited point of view. Plus almost all of those are complete sentences, and I haven't made up a single word.

I count that as progress.

Here's a bit more:

I see it coming. My mother maneuvers the Corvair too close to a line of parked cars and bounces off the side fender of someone's station wagon. Again, the Corvair skids on the ice and comes to a stop in the middle of the road.

"Shit," she whispers. "My luck."

"Let's walk," I say again. "Leave the car here."

"I'm fine," my mother insists, but even at ten I can tell that she is straining to sound calm, in control. "Just have to go more slowly."

One last time, my mother moves the car along the whitened pavement, but the snow grows thicker, and I can barely see to the end of the hood. "I better park," she admits finally. "I think I hit someone's car."

I try by sheer mental will to direct the Corvair into one of the slanted parking spaces outside the Five and Dime. My mother manages to aim well enough into the slot, but isn't able to find the brake until the front half of the car is up over the curb and onto the sidewalk.

"Why?" she moans. "Why does it always have to snow?"

I see a red light flashing into the car and turn around in my seat; a black-and-white cruiser is directly behind us, and a man is already stepping out of the driver-side door. He comes around, aims his flashlight beam into the glass of my mother's window.

She rolls the window down. "Should have seen this coming," she mutters.

The officer stands slightly back, at attention, the flashlight beam held steady. In the dark, with the snow, and his light in our eyes, I can tell nothing about him except that he is tall.

"Marge," he says.

"Tom," my mother answers. It is a small town. We all know one another.

As verified by no less an authority than Google Maps, I met George Plimpton when I was a young man, spent many hours driving the Lion of New Journalism over Pittsburgh's bridges and through its claustrophobic tunnels. I can't be sure what he said to me because I was stoned then as well. But maybe he said something like this:

"So, kid, if you really want to tell the truth, just write fiction. Memoir is for wieners. Do you want to be a wiener?"[1]

I *didn't* want to be a wiener, and that's why I wrote my story as fiction.

Do you want to be a wiener?

Does your wiener have a first name?

> ### Helpful Writing Prompt
> Write a truthful memory of your life. Then change key details to give the story more flow, and rearrange the chronology of events to create a far more graceful and pleasing narrative arc. At the top of the first page, write: Fiction.

Telling the Truth in Personal Memoir Tip 3
Remember: You Can't Make This Shit Up

Many years later, Plimpton's prediction turned out to be false. I had become neither a wiener nor a fiction writer, but one of America's Most Respected Obscure Memoirists.

Believe me, I wear this badge with pride.

As a Respected but Obscure American Memoirist, it seemed there was a need for me to write about stuff that really happened—

---

1. Some of these details may be misremembered.

using my own name and honest-to-goodness details. What's that all about?

So anyway, I recycled the snowstorm story once again, but this time I told it straight, unemblemmed, and defictionalized.

Here is what came out:

> My memory is of careening through a blizzard one Christmas Eve, my mother at the wheel. No one should have been out driving that night, given the visibility, but more to the point, my mother was drunk—so bombed that she eventually scraped the front bumper of our family Chevy across the side panels of two or three parked cars.
>
> I was six or so. "Don't worry," my mother kept telling me. "I'm all right."
>
> But she wasn't, and she knew it.
>
> We were a block from our house when it finally dawned on Mom that skimming metal to metal against a line of parked cars was not acceptable, no matter how much snow was falling, or what the holiday. Her response was to drive two miles out of her way, straight down snow-drifted West 8th Street, to the City Hall police station. Once there, she turned herself in.
>
> The officers behind the desk, perhaps already caught up in their own Christmas Eve revelry, seemed to find my mother's predicament amusing. I don't remember, but I'm guessing they took down the pertinent information. Or maybe they didn't. It was Christmas, after all.

Thus, we have come full circle.

And the lesson here, my writer friends?

If you want to write good, use empty transitional phrases like "thus, we have come full circle," because even though these phrases may be meaningless, they sound awfully nice, and people often nod thoughtfully in response, because the words are soothing and familiar.

> **Helpful Writing Prompt**
> Consider this: If you were a wiener, if that is what you'd truly love to be, the whole world, with the likely exception of Muslims, kosher Jews, vegetarians, vegans, devout Hindus, and those on low-salt diets, would truly be in love with you. Now freewrite for thirty minutes from the point of view of an all-beef tube of meat. Take your freewriting and turn it into a memoir entitled *Pray Love, Don't Eat Me!*

Telling the Truth in Personal Memoir Tip 4
Remember: Two Moments and a Sense of Powerlessness

It is now roughly thirty-three years since I wrote the words "*occurrences are not alone and we are not apart from that which does occur*" and I still don't understand them.

It is roughly twenty-three years since I subsequently wrote the short story based on my mother's drunk driving escapade. (And I still don't understand her.)

It is roughly eight years since I took this memory and attempted to recreate it in memoir.

What do I really remember?

I have what I believe to be a reliable memory of a moment—almost a flash, a photographic instant—on Eighth Street, in my hometown, in a heavy snowstorm. I can see through my six-year-old eyes the cars parked along the north side of the road, and I remember my fear and confusion when my mother chose to drive on to the police station. I have a second flash of memory: the one where we are pulling in front of our house, on Ninth Street, in a police cruiser, and hoping that none of the neighbors will be looking out their window and witnessing the latest Moore family embarrassment.

I have an emotional memory as well, of feeling powerless. I probably—though, in truth, now I am out of the realm of verifiable memory and well into speculation, but speculation based on knowing very well what sort of a boy I was back then—said something like, "Mom, is that a good idea?" just quietly enough that she could ignore me if she wished.

Which she did, more or less. I feel pretty sure that she answered me—"Don't worry, I'm okay"—but she kept driving.

That's about it.

Those two moments and a sense of powerlessness. The rest, I remember remembering, years later, years ago, when I pieced it all together in my mind.

Memory is like a rope, knotted every three or four feet, and hanging down a deep well. When you pull it up, just about anything might be attached to those knots. But you'll never know what's there if you don't pull. And the more you pull at that rope, the more you find.

Your memory rope may not contain a precise, photographic accounting of past events, because those moments become lost within seconds of anything that occurs. But still, your honest (if not accurate) memories will be attached to those knots, and those honest memories—along with reflection, examination, reconsideration—are precisely what the memoirist has to offer.

> ### *Helpful Writing Prompt*
> Enroll immediately in a summer writing workshop on some pastoral, semiabandoned liberal arts campus, one with benches and trees. Study "The Art of Memoir" with a Respected but Obscure American Memoirist. Ask repeatedly, "What *is* creative about creative nonfiction? Doesn't 'creative' mean that I *can* change things?" Wait until the instructor collapses backward in his or her chair, defeated, ready to abandon all hope of ever explaining to you what is truthful about memoir, and then smile broadly and shout, "I was *only* kidding, silly goose!"

Meaningless Concluding Paragraphs
Remember that the time and energy you invest in your memoir doesn't end once you revise the final page, or even after the manuscript has been edited, produced, and published. There are lawsuits yet to come, plus lengthy interviews to be posted on blogs that no one ever reads.

And here are some final tips:

- Supercharge your memoir with strong verbs and electro-magnetic nouns.
- Use adverbs rarely and sparingly.
- Add twelve spaces after each period.   Readers will be impressed by the length of your book.
- If you are a movie star, be sure to mention that on page 1.
- Emblemmed is not a word.
- Avoid familiar metaphors like the plague.
- Avoid the plague.
- Readers love sex, so consider traveling house to house with your book and a gigantic pack of condoms.

Remember, too, that the role of a writer is not to say what we all can say, but to say what we all can say in such a way that the writer garners the interest of a high-powered literary agent.

When writing long passages of exposition, consider using abbreviations.

And finally, remember that if you don't tell your story, no one will.

Which might be just fine.

A Question from
PATRICK MADDEN

Mister Essay Writer Guy

Dear Mister Essay Writer Guy,

My friend Chris Arthur was telling me recently about a poet who was mining his [Arthur's] essays for "found poems," with some interesting results. Chris wondered about the question of originality/creativity/authorship, saying, "I guess she's the poet and I'm—what? Maybe the beach to her beachcomber?"

In Uruguay, the English word "beachcomber" has become *bichicome*, a synonym for "indigent," "layabout," or "bum." But I think that essays themselves are all and always "found," to varying degrees, what with their reliance on factual experience and information, their emphasis on cobbling together thought and story from external reality, so are essayists all *bichicomes?*

Patrick Madden
Provo, Utah

Dear Patrick,

If I were to say that all essayists were bitchy-somethings, do you think it would hurt my popularity?

I've established earlier in this sagacious essay compendium that Montaigne was an indigent and a bum, albeit a wealthy one, and to be entirely honest, I've got my doubts about you and a lot of other people represented in this book, given that I asked you to send me questions and everyone responded so promptly and nicely.

Really, don't you have better things to do?

Now *I'm* being bitchy.

Here's a found essay, by the way. I found it on my answering machine. That's a little more creative than finding your "found essay" or "found poem" in a literary magazine, don't you think? I don't know your friend Chris Arthur, but if he wants to fight, I'm standing at the ready.

In extreme bitch mode,

Mister Essay Writer Guy

The Actual Message Mike the Tree Guy Left on My Answering Machine the Evening I Arrived Home to Find that the Tree He Was Cutting Down When I Left for Work That Morning Still Stood Tall in My Side Yard

Hi, this is Mike the tree guy.

You may have noticed that I didn't take your tree down today.

It's hard to explain exactly what happened, except I found myself up in your extremely rotten tree, out on a limb hanging over the street, with all of these cars passing below me, and I had what some might call a moment of clarity:

I need to find a new job.

So that may be the last tree I ever climb. I don't know.

So, anyway, sorry for the inconvenience. Bye.

A Question from
STEVE ALMOND

Mister Essay Writer Guy

Dear Mister Essay Writer Guy,

I keep reading articles on the Internet saying that memoirs and autobiographical essays are the devil's work. Does this mean I am the devil? If so, why do I look so silly in red? Also, why don't I earn more overtime? How does Oprah fit into all this? I'm holding my breath until you answer.

Steve Almond

Boston, Massachusetts

Dear Steve,

The real problem is not that memoirists are the devil, or that you look lousy in red, but that I couldn't get a date as a young man and my feelings remain hurt. Do you think it is possible that Lisa and Mary Carole realized that I was going to be a memoirist, and chose to date other boys for that very reason?

Otherwise, I would be writing about them a lot more than I already have.

By my calculation, you have been holding your breath for eighteen months at this point. So let me get right to my answer.

Exhale,

Mister Essay Writer Guy

An Essay on the Inherent Dangers of Memoir Writing

There was a time when you had to earn the right to draft a memoir, by accomplishing something noteworthy or having an extremely unusual experience. . . . But then came our current age of oversharing, and all heck broke loose.

—NEAL GENZLINGER,
NEW YORK TIMES BOOK REVIEW

I don't mean to overshare here, but I wrote a memoir once, and all hell did not break loose.[1]

---

1. DISCLAIMER: Some people have had changes in behavior, hostility, agitation, depressed mood, suicidal thoughts or actions while using MEMOIR to help them examine their lives. Some people had these symptoms when they began writing MEMOIR, and others developed them after several weeks of freewriting and electromagnetic noun replacement. If you, your family, or your writing workshop leader notice agitation, hostility, depression, or changes in behavior, thinking, or mood that are not typical for you, or you develop suicidal thoughts or actions, anxiety, panic, aggression, genital warts, or genre confusion, or if you begin to obsess day and night over the best ways to gain the attention of a well-placed literary agent, stop writing MEMOIR and call your doctor right away. Also tell your doctor about any history of SHORT FICTION or POETICS. Do not write MEMOIR if you have had serious allergic or skin reactions after bathing in bourbon. The most common side effects of MEMOIR include nausea, sleep problems, constipation, gas, and swelling of the navel. If you have side effects that bother you or don't go away, tell your doctor promptly. He likely won't care one bit. He is working on his memoir. You may have vivid, unusual, or strange dreams while writing MEMOIR. Write them down. Do not operate a tractor or other heavy equipment while writing MEMOIR, unless you are writing a chapter set on your family farm. MEMOIR should not be combined with other forms of writing, such as poetry, skin art, or ransom notes. You may need a lower dose of MEMOIR if you have relatives with excellent memory skills, or legal representation. Before starting MEMOIR, tell your workshop leader if you are pregnant, plan to become pregnant, or are taking the summer workshop in the hopes of having an extramarital affair. If you find yourself in an unsavory, brief sexual relationship as a result of taking MEMOIR, capture the minute details in scenic form.

A Question from
ANDER MONSON

Mister Essay Writer Guy

Dear Mister Essay Writer Guy,

When I was in grad school, I took linguistics with the overly alliterative Dr. Dan Douglas, as he preferred not to be called. Instead he asked us to call him Dan. Unsurprisingly, he wore shorts exclusively, year-round. This was in the upper Midwest where it snows. He sat back in his chair. He was chill. I didn't work very hard in his class, and didn't understand as much as I might have: I was still in my lazy student mode. Perhaps because of my northern Scandinavian blood, I've always been a warm-blooded fellow. In this way, sartorially, shorts have always appealed to me. We're not talking short-shorts, but not capris either. But the risk of wearing shorts, aside from being more susceptible to contact with plants, pets, and chapping, is becoming the guy who always wears shorts. Now I teach my own class. I wear shorts a lot, this being Arizona. I've taken to wearing golf shirts too. I've been writing shorts now and I know you do too. Dan gave me an A– in the class. I suspect he didn't believe in penalizing idiocy too strongly. Should I have received a lower grade? Should I stop wearing or writing shorts? And what are the risks of being the guy who always wears or writes shorts?

Ander Monson
Tucson, Arizona

Dear Ander,

Yes, you should stop wearing shorts when you teach.

Yes, your students paid me to say so.

Also, shorts are important.

No less a writer than Nelson Algren taught me that.

Briefly,

Mister Essay Writer Guy

Nelson Algren's Shorts

For always our villains have hearts of gold
and all our heroes are slightly tainted.
—NELSON ALGREN

Nelson Algren answered my knock with a low, tired groan.

"Hang on," he eventually muttered through a thick wooden door. "One minute."

The Chicago novelist was visiting the University of Pittsburgh to speak with young writing majors. It was April 1977, and I was one of these young writers, and Algren's student escort as well. I had been instructed to do whatever it was that our honored guest desired, so I waited dutifully in the hallway outside of his hotel room and practiced what I would say when he came to the door.

Algren, author of novels like *A Walk on the Wild Side* and *Man with a Golden Arm*, winner of the 1950 National Book Award, had been called the best contemporary author after William Faulkner. Hemingway himself said that, so I knew it had to be true. And Algren's reputation extended beyond his writing. He made his name chronicling the seamier sides of Chicago—the pimps, prostitutes, petty thieves, con men, addicts, derelicts, and cheats. Algren was rumored to be part of the action, a bit of a tough guy himself.

Maybe we would search out Pittsburgh's secret crap games and wily bookmakers, I thought as I waited outside his door that morning. Maybe we would place a few smart bets. My plan was to just stay quiet and put my money where Algren put his.

Or perhaps, it occurred to me, we would simply screw the top off a pint of rye and sit along the copper-colored Monongahela River. He would tell some stories, offer some advice.

My wait in that hallway extended far beyond the one minute Algren had suggested.

A grown man could have shaved and dressed in the time I stood waiting.

Probably, one did.

When the heavy door swung open, the man facing me looked much older than the book jacket picture I had carefully scrutinized in the weeks leading up to Algren's visit. The novelist's green suit was worn, oversized, begging for a dry cleaner. He wore white socks with brown shoes. His face was pale, his eyes slightly yellow, and he rather needed a haircut.

I'd expected movie star good looks. Gold watches and diamond pinkie rings. An Italian suit at the very least.

But looks can be deceiving, I reminded myself.

Forgetting in the moment my carefully prepared introductory speech, the one where I made it clear to him that I was something special, not just some college kid escort but a college kid escort who was going to be a real writer someday, I managed to utter a mere "Hello, Mr. Algren."

Then: "What would you like to do today, Mr. Algren?"

My voice was chirpy, I think, rather than authoritative. Though my goal was to appear both worldly and eager, I'm sure I came off as simply silly.

But I caught myself, remembered my purpose, and screwed up enough nerve to speak a third time. I informed Algren that I owned a car, and that we had the entire afternoon and early evening free.

Algren reached down, pulled up the hand I had been too nervous to extend his way, and shook it firmly.

"I want to buy underwear," he growled. "Take me somewhere I can buy some shorts."

For a moment, I just didn't respond. Was he speaking in code? My mind tried to put together underwear with something daring and incorrigible, something more in keeping with the world of Algren's books. Maybe the underwear would be ladies' underwear, and still on the ladies? Perhaps "shorts" meant something different in Chicago from what it does in Pittsburgh?

Eventually, I managed a firm, "Excuse me?"

"I need to go someplace and buy underwear. I don't have a single clean pair."

"Underwear, Mr. Algren?"

"Yeah. Shorts."

Algren and I set off, on foot, for a Woolworth's 5 & 10 that morning.

As we ambled along Forbes Avenue, I tossed out a few astute facts about the campus buildings we passed, but clearly he wasn't interested. Algren walked at a steady clip for a man in his late sixties. This surprised me, being twenty-one and ignorant.

"Are we close?" he asked after about five minutes.

"Just one more block."

This seemed to please him, and he smiled slightly the rest of the walk.

We entered Woolworth's, which was very much like entering the past. The store was on its last legs, dimly lit, poorly staffed, an eager candidate for urban renewal. We stepped down three short steps to the retail area, and the Famous American Novelist snatched the first package of men's shorts he saw. Three white boxers, about a 36 waist.

I hung back, embarrassed, not wanting anyone to connect me with the old man.

"Now take me home," he said.

We retraced our steps briskly, me holding in my disappointment and Algren hugging his Woolworth's bag. Along the way, scanning the businesses lining Forbes, Algren spotted Frankie Gustine's, a smoky tavern named for a former Pirates infielder. He knew the name.

Algren suddenly wanted a drink. So we went in.

I asked for a beer.

"Bring the boy a martini," Algren ordered the bartender.

"Excuse me?" I asked, but no one was listening, least of all the fellow behind the bar, who seemed to sense immediately that this was not some old man with a bag full of boxers, but a man of some consequence and gravity.

When the drinks came, in tall-stemmed, chilled glasses, Algren showed his first real interest in me. "You had one of these before?" he asked.

"No," I said.

He seemed fascinated with this idea, the boy and his first martini, and eyed me closely while I sipped, demanded to know my reaction immediately.

I lied and said the drink was good, though in truth it tasted to me like vinegar and urine. I regret to this day that I didn't tell him that. He might have laughed.

We had one martini each, and Algren lectured me on why a martini was the proper thing to drink. His reasoning had to do with the seriousness of drinking. A real drink was a real drink, while a beer was just water with a little bit of booze mixed in. "You look like an amateur," he warned me.

I was, and mostly we sat in silence, studying the back of the bar. There wasn't much a man like Algren could possibly want to know about a green college kid writer, and I could no longer imagine what questions I might ask him.

At the bottom of the drink, Algren said, "Finished."

So we exited and walked back toward his room, slightly drunk. I was slightly drunk, that is. I don't know about Algren. His step had slowed some, he was still quiet, but he was probably fine.

I followed him into the Webster Hall lobby, into the elevator, and up to his floor, and then stood outside the big wooden door again. He shook my hand, assured me he would find his way to the student union that evening entirely on his own.

I was about to go, but he had some trouble with the key and the lock. My hand was steadier, so I opened the door for him, watched his back as he ambled into the surprisingly small and shabby room. I remember feeling embarrassed that we had put him there. A remarkable man like this deserves a nicer room. And a better escort. And someone with a better sense of what he might need. He was not the man I had imagined he would be. He was just a writer of enormous talent.

After the door was opened, Algren turned my way one last time. "Thanks," he said. "I had a good time."

He was across the room, undressing for his nap, before I even shut the door.

A Question from
BRENDA MILLER

Mister Essay Writer Guy

Dear Mister Essay Writer Guy,

When I post something on Facebook, I sometimes feel like Sally Field gushing, "You like me; right now, you like me!" I'll check frequently to see how many likes or comments I get, and feel a silly flush of pride when there's lots, and crestfallen when there's none. I feel like I'm back in seventh grade, shuffling along the edge of the chain-link fence, waiting for someone to notice me and then either (a) too eager when they do or (b) humiliated when they don't.

I know you might tell me I should just leave the playground altogether, but it's where all the cool kids are. It's the only place, these days, where I can find out about babies being born and dogs dying. It's the babble of a party going on in the next room. It's like one big communal personal essay I can't stop reading.

Which leads me to my question. Or maybe two questions. Now that we're becoming acclimated to this scrolling public broadsheet crying out the village news, does this alter the role of the personal essay writer? I mean, does anyone really care about the personal essay anymore, when everyone is already on display? And how do we shut the door on the party long enough to think our own thoughts without reflexively wondering if we'll be "liked"? I think (though this could be totally false) that I did my best writing long ago, when I assumed I wouldn't even be read, much less "liked." There's something about talking to yourself, rather than to the thumbnailed crowd, that seems more authentic to me.

Or am I just the geeky kid whining on the sidelines?

Thanks, Mister Essay Writer Guy,

Brenda Miller
Bellingham, Washington

Dear Brenda,

Anecdotal evidence shows that many a contemporary writer has trouble avoiding the wordplay, entertainment value, and immediate gratification of Facebook status updates, while at the same time the endemic shallowness and attention-depleting atmosphere results in countless choruses of "I'm trying to spend less time here . . . but I can't seem to tear myself away."

For my part, the first six months of 2010 were spent riding just such a pathetic wave, vacillating between the posting of thoughtful quotes about writing (as if this were somehow justification for the time I was reading Facebook and *not* writing) and giving myself over entirely to the utter and endless nonsense.

Can a chronological string of Facebook wall postings create a narrative?

If so, then maybe I was writing all along, despite myself. If not, then I need to find a new excuse. Though I've edited away much of the repetition and detritus, what you read on the next few pages represents an accurate, purely chronological, and possibly embarrassing chronicle of the time I've wasted. You should know: you were there.

In a cautioning tone,

Mister Essay Writer Guy

Why I Trained My Dog to Post

One Writer's Facebook Journey

The sublime and the ridiculous are
often so nearly related that it is difficult
to class them separately.
—THOMAS PAINE

Dinty W Moore Hello to all of my auld acquaintances. You
are often brought to mind.
December 31 at 7:51am • Like • Comment • Share

George Hartley well lang my syne

Richard Hoffman A cup 'o kindness to ya.

Dinty W Moore has a happy Facebook story to share:
I found a silver ring in the Philadelphia airport on 12/30,
with a distinctive name inscribed inside the band, and sure
enough found someone with that name through Facebook.
She lost it, had "given up hope," and was thrilled that
it had been found, due to sentimental value. I mailed it to
her today. So Facebook can be good for more than just
jokes, maybe?
January 2 at 12:22pm • Like • Comment • Share

Halvard Johnson You're telling us that this place has some
practical uses?

Elizabeth Kadetsky . . . and then you got married?

Dinty W Moore Am I bothered? Do I look bothered?
January 5 at 8:54am • Like • Comment • Share

David Kirby You look bewitched and bewildered, Dinty, but not bothered.

Dinty W Moore's head will explode in 5, 4, 3, 2 . . .
January 12 at 5:44am • Like • Comment • Share

Rhonda L. M. Tipton Was that what that was? I thought the local rock quarry was blasting again.

Jane Satterfield Are you sure it's not in 4, 8, 15, 16, 23, 42?

Dinty W Moore would (also) really like to have one of those celebrity-style nervous breakdowns where you can't take it anymore and you're rushed to a luxury spa to recuperate while other people take care of everything for you.
January 12 at 1:22pm • Like • Comment • Share

Melanie Sumner I have always wanted one of those nervous breakdowns! First I was too poor, and then I was too poor and had kids. But I'm not giving up.

Zoe Forney You can come to my house!

Dinty W Moore "It's so interesting because people do feel they know me after reading my essays, and I appreciate that. But at the same time they don't know me; they know the person on the page. It's a very real persona, but it's not the entirety of who I am, so it can be a little tricky."— Essayist Brenda Miller on persona
February 1 at 7:53am • Like • Comment • Share

Robin Hemley Next time I see you and Brenda . . . I suggest we send our personae off to the movies or something while our true selves have lunch. What do you say?

Dinty W Moore wants Facebook to switch him to the new homepage design, so that he too can start complaining about it.
February 6 at 8:43am • Like • Comment • Share

Dinty W Moore and Josh Russell are now friends.
• Like • Comment • Share • View Feedback

Josh Russell Wait, I'm confused, we weren't already FB pals? This machine confuses me.

Dinty W Moore wonders whether those brave men and women who settled the American West used to march out onto the streets of Dodge City and shoot their sidearms into the air whenever the wi-fi went down in Kitty's Saloon.
February 9 at 9:35am • Like • Comment • Share

James Irwin thinks Dinty is playing around too much with his profile picture and status, and obviously needs more to do to keep him busy.

February 9 at 9:46am • Like • Comment • Share • View Feedback • See Wall-to-Wall

Dinty W Moore "Poetry, after all, is a bird, and prose, as we know, is a potato. Nice that we can all agree on something." —Billy Collins

February 18 at 7:10am • Like • Comment • Share

Jackson Connor Lucky for us, we're having chicken and homefries for dinner tonight—we'll be eating a prose poem—yum.

Dinty W Moore Scratch here ▇▇▇▇▇▇▇ to reveal today's highly amazing writing advice.

February 23 at 9:32pm • Like • Comment • Share

Grace Lovelace I won large fries!

Mike Lorden Can you just tell us? I don't want that stuff all over my screen.

David Sanders . . . a little higher and to the left.

Dinty W Moore "A good many young writers make the mistake of enclosing a stamped, self-addressed envelope, big enough for the manuscript to come back in. This is too much of a temptation to the editor." —Ring Lardner

February 25 at 9:47am • Like • Comment • Share

Dinty W Moore "The key to a successful writing career is to be born brilliant, with flawless work habits, little need for sleep, and wealthy grandparents who own prestigious magazines and publishing houses." —D. William Moore
March 11 at 8:54am • Like • Comment • Share

Dinty W Moore Everybody here in Tuscaloosa is sure fond of that one brand of laundry detergent.
March 24 at 5:01pm • Like • Comment • Share

Leslie F. Miller You know why I wash my clothes in Tide? Because it's too cold out tide.

Dinty W Moore never updated his status from an airport before, but it seems so jet-set when others do it, so here I am, in Charlotte International, feeling all George Clooney–like.
March 27 at 1:21pm • Like • Comment • Share

Dinty W Moore Somebody with exquisite timing should schedule an interview with Gay Talese soon, only to find when they show up that he has a persistent cold.
March 28 at 3:36pm • Like • Comment • Share

Jeff Gundy What's really scary is that I get this.

Dinty W Moore is leaving Facebook for good. Also shutting down his e-mail. If you want to send me a message, mail me here: Dinty W. Moore, 1 April Lane, Athens, OH 45701.
April 1 at 7:46am • Like • Comment • Share

Laura Orem Say it ain't so!

Elisa Tuning Rodgers But I just found you! Rats!!!

Ned Stuckey-French No, no, no!

Marc Snyder 1 April Lane, huh?

Catherine Taylor My youngest, Emrys, is selling nuts in a can. Want some?

Dinty W Moore To everyone who fell for my April Fool's gag: hello, I'm back. To everyone else: hello.
April 2 at 6:51am • Like • Comment • Share

Dinty W Moore "My job is not to just set down events that happened to me. My job is to create an experience for a reader." —Mary Karr
April 4 at 8:45pm • Like • Comment • Share

Halvard Johnson I say just give the readers the materials and let them create their own experience(s).

Dinty W Moore is surrounded by 6,000 writers, 400 editors, and a big blue bear.
April 7 at 8:15pm • Like • Comment • Share

Stephanie Kartalopoulos me too. me too. me too . . .

Erik Blair Odds are the Bear gets all the chicks . . .

Ira Sukrungruang How can two debonair big men like us not meet this entire weekend? I still owe you a beer!
April 11 at 12:55am • Like • Comment • Share • See Wall-to-Wall

 Dinty W Moore Aw shucks!
April 12 at 10:08pm • Like • Comment • Share

Dinty W Moore "Don't be afraid to be confused. Try to remain permanently confused. . . . Stay open, forever, so open it hurts, and then open up some more, until the day you die, world without end, amen." —George Saunders
April 15 at 8:28am • Like • Comment • Share

Sherrie Flick Nice.

Laura Orem I don't understand . . .

Dinty W Moore "Dinty's Saturday Status Update," Based on the Novel "Push" by Sapphire
April 17 at 9:25am • Like • Comment • Share

Paul Jones I guess it's going to be a hell of a Saturday.

 Dinty W Moore "Language alone protects us from the scariness of things with no names." —Toni Morrison
April 28 at 9:00am • Like • Comment • Share

Erik Blair Yeah, I call my dog "Knuckle-head" because I'm afraid not too :)

Iwan Sitompul Greetings from Ubud, the cultural center of Baliness people and thank you for the add.
May 1 at 7:22am • Like • Comment • Share • See Wall-to-Wall

Dinty W Moore "I'm a writer, so I don't wait for something interesting. I write. Period. And if there's nothing interesting, I'll make it interesting." —Thomas Lynch
May 4 at 7:20pm • Like • Comment • Share

Elmo Daffington Jr. You betcha!

Joy Gaines-Friedler Had a Dinty Moore at the deli yesterday—seriously. Corned beef with Russian dressing! Thanks for all the quotes on writing—love them. Joy
May 5 at 10:32am • Like • Comment • Share • See Wall-to-Wall

Dinty W Moore "The writer of nonfiction might be starting with events that really happened, but recreating them is an imaginative feat. Ordering them is an imaginative feat. Making sense of them is an imaginative feat." —Robin Hemley
May 6 at 8:39am • Like • Comment • Share

 Dinty W Moore "To live is so startling, it leaves little time for anything else." —Emily Dickinson
May 7 at 8:38am • Like • Comment • Share

Dave Bonta If by "live" she means "hang out on Facebook," I couldn't agree more.

Dinty W Moore "A poet is someone who stands outside in the rain hoping to be struck by lightning." —James Dickey
May 12 at 8:32am • Like • Comment • Share

Rodger Kamenetz No, a poet is someone who stands outside on a perfectly clear day and hopes to be struck by a butterfly.

Kirk Nesset Fiction writers, likewise, stand around waiting for the careening cement truck.

Dinty W Moore Creative nonfiction writers stand outside in the rain hoping to be struck by Oprah.

Susan M. Schultz James Dickey was a poet who was struck too often by what he thought was lightning.

Dinty W Moore I think Dickey was struck by white lightning.

Dinty W Moore "It's hell writing and it's hell not writing. The only tolerable state is having just written." —Robert Hass
May 22 at 11:59am • Like • Comment • Share

Terry Savoie Exactly! Right now I'm in the tolerable state. That will end in about an hour or so. Then it's back to hell.

Stephen Kuusisto This is why I trained my dog to write.

Dinty W Moore ". . . permit me to say without reservation that if all people were attentive, if they would undertake to be attentive every moment of their lives, they would discover the world anew." —Jacques Lusseyran
May 26 at 9:20am • Like • Comment • Share

Mary Jo Cartledgehayes I'm sorry. Could you repeat that, please? I was daydreaming.

 Dinty W Moore is worried that Facebook is eating his brain.
May 26 at 11:45am • Like • Comment • Share

Susanne Nan Bayes Koenig That's what that burp was this morning when I logged on . . . thanks for explaining it, Dinty.

Dana Guthrie Martin more like digesting and distributing across a relatively small subnetwork

Paul Morris Brains . . . with fava beans and a nice chianti. . . .

Lori Rohlk Pfeiffer That's food for thought.

Dinty W Moore "What crazies we writers are, our heads full of language like buckets of minnows standing in the moonlight on a dock" —Hayden Carruth
May 27 at 10:53am · Comment · Like · View Feedback

Anne Desarro the hardest thing is catching the minnows . . . once they are in the bucket you are halfway home

Dinty W Moore There is not time enough in the day for Facebook and work, so I'm taking the advice of Stephen Kuusisto and training my dog to write. But here's the vexing question: do I train Buster the Wonder Dog to write my books, or train him to do my daily status updates? I'm torn.

May 28 at 9:36am · Comment · Like · View Feedback

Krystal Knapp Important question. Has Buster been taught about the privacy settings on Facebook and how not to reveal all your private information to the world?

Dinty W Moore bark. bark. woof.

May 29 at 8:32am · Comment · Like · View Feedback

Beth Foulkes Lowe Concise. To the point. A good start. Heh.

Kim Aubrey Your dog is doing a great job!

Elizabeth Edmonson Great start, but I think he needs help with capitalization, Dinty.

Judith Barrington doggerel?

Kate Fox Yes. Sit. Stay. Good dog.

A Question from
DAVID SHIELDS

Mister Essay Writer Guy

Dear Essay Guy Dude,

In one koan-like sentence, track for me the connection between Buddhism and writing.

David Shields
Seattle, Washington

Dear David,

First, let me tell you a small story about my introduction to Buddhism?

Twenty some years ago, in response to an advertisement in a small weekly newspaper, I appeared at the doorway of Lily Wong for personal instruction.

Even at first glance, it was obvious that my teacher must have changed her name at some point—she had not a hint of Asian heritage in her eyes, her skin tones, or her speech. She was blonde and pink.

This was during the time that the phrase "New Age" was bandied about to describe everything from deep Eastern philosophy to past-life regression and lacquered stones. Ms. Wong's Philadelphia townhouse exhibited evidence of all of these, and being a skeptical young man, distrustful of anything faddish, I almost turned around and left the front room when I saw the aromatherapy candles. But I didn't.

For the next five weeks, Lily Wong instructed me, along with four other ragtag beginners, in various forms of meditation and breathing. The format was always similar: we would assemble on Monday evenings, write Ms. Wong a check, march up the steps to her third floor, and sit on plush purple cushions while she instructed us on the finer points of breathing and visualization. The attic room was filled with incense.

Lily would not stay with us after the thirty minutes of instruction, but instead would disappear downstairs, returning forty or fifty minutes later to strike the bell that signaled the return to normal activity. I was naïve enough at this time not to realize how irregular it was for the teacher to not join in meditation. I figured maybe she had reached enlightenment some months earlier, so sitting with us would just be a waste of her time?

It took a fair amount of concentration and willpower for the five newcomers to remain on our cushions for that hour-and-a-half—ninety minutes can seem an eternity when you are stuck in one place with nothing to do—but that is why we were there. So we endured.

But then one night—the fifth week, I believe—I had consumed too much water with my premeditation dinner, and my bladder karma was too strong to be avoided. Halfway through the sitting portion of the evening, I rose from my pillow and tiptoed downstairs to find the bathroom in this exotic stranger's home.

As luck would have it, I opened the wrong door.

Inside the spare bedroom, Lily was sitting on a futon sofa with her thirteen-year-old son, smoking marijuana and watching a Road Runner cartoon.

The coyote was just about to go off the end of the butte.

And I was enlightened.

Namaste,

Mister Essay Writer Guy

Beep! Beep!

Life is full of discontent, the Buddha told us, and that discontent stems from our grasping, our craving and clinging, our desire to make permanent what will always be fleeting, which is all well and good, and brilliant, and wise beyond saying, but the grasping and craving and clinging is also the definition of the authentic writing life—the wicked desire to say something worthwhile, the unquenchable yearning to make permanent in ink and paper the fleeting moments that constitute the universal human experience—so what the heck, I ask myself, how can I possibly embrace the teachings of the Buddha (which I do) and still ignore them for two, three, four hours a day while sitting at my writing desk, clinging, craving, trying to pin down elusive sentences with a desperation resembling that dang-burned coyote trying to pin down the road runner; which brings me to a story of sorts, a true story, though it never happened, and thus a parable, a parable that begins like this: a monk, we'll call him Wi-Lee—*yes, that's it*, Wi-Lee Coyote—asks Mister Sensei Essay Writer Guy, "How can we escape the moments when the writing doesn't flow?" and Mister Sensei Essay Writer Guy opens his eyes momentarily, smiles, and says, "When you are not writing, be thoroughly not writing; when you are writing, be writing through and through."[1]

---

1. And then the anvil drops.

A Question from
ROXANE GAY

Mister Essay Writer GuY

Dear Mister Essay Writer Guy,

Why do so many writers only write about writing? Why do they act like writing is the only thing? What about writing about writing makes writers think they are writing something worth reading? Your assistance in this matter would be greatly appreciated.

Yours, in writing,

Roxane Gay
West Lafayette, Indiana

Dear Roxane,

Given the subject matter of this book, I feel personally attacked by your question.

But that's okay. I like the attention.

Basking,

Mister Essay Writer Guy

Don't Read This Essay

1. New York City, December: Union laborers with crowbars and sledgehammers are ripping out wallboard in the hotel room just above us. My teaching colleague Kate and I are in the midtown Hilton, attempting to ignore the noise, struggling to remain focused on the schedule of hopeful candidates interviewing for a faculty opening in rhetoric and composition.

2. I am keeping this essay brief on purpose. Feel free to skim.

3. One by one, the fresh-faced applicants in their postmodern eyewear enter the hotel room, sit in the one available chair, and explain the various ways they teach what we once called "freshman English." Each of these applicants—they are bright, from good schools, with impressive depths of knowledge— outlines an innovative new assignment they give their students in first-year writing classes. One favors a service-learning project, sending out students to work in an underprivileged Chicago neighborhood. Another hands her students disposable cameras so they "can learn to construct an argument out of the pictures they take." A third sends her students to welfare offices, to "examine the discourse" of filling out forms.

4. The idea that students don't know how to write clearly and precisely is as old as school itself, probably, but lately it seems as if students no longer know how to read either. It is true on my campus, and from what I can gather, on many other college campuses. The students understand words, sentences—they are not illiterate—but they don't seem to grasp the *reasons* for

reading. They seem baffled when asked to take two thoughts, connect them, and form something new. They read James Baldwin or Henry David Thoreau and their primary reaction seems to be, "Okay, now I've read that. I'm done."

5. As if the only goal in reading was to have looked at every word.

6. Pessimists, of course, have been predicting the death of the literature for nearly as long as the literature has existed.

7. The din of construction from the Hilton Towers' twenty-second floor suggests an ongoing battle between an inebriated rhino and a disoriented hippopotamus. Kate and I call the front desk, but no one can compel union laborers to give up overtime and go home—certainly not in Manhattan. The job applicants who file through our room are brave about the unrelenting noise, but also flustered. Kate and I apologize profusely. At times, we have to cease conversation and just shrug.

8. I ask one of the candidates—the one who sends her students into impoverished Chicago neighborhoods to do service learning—the $64,000 question: "So they do this work in the neighborhoods, right? And then they write papers about their experiences?"

9. There is a brief pause, and then a brief answer. A very vague answer. This is a job interview, so the young woman understandably hedges her bets. We all smile and let the moment pass.

10. So, students aren't actually writing in their writing classes? Has it come to this?

11. I want to blame television. I want to blame standardized testing. I want to blame the Internet.

12. I want to blame my colleagues who teach discourse communities, multimodal composition, and intertextuality instead of how to make oneself clear on the page.

13. I want to blame literary theorists who make reading such a complex, disconnected, destructive chore.

14. I'm looking for someone to blame.

15. Notice how I've numbered the sections here, and kept them brief? I'm hoping this will help even the reluctant reader to digest the material. One could, for instance, read just one section a day, and be done within a month.

16. As the interviews progress, I begin to catch on. The applicants for our composition position have been tutored by their graduate school mentors to give their students only cursory reading assignments. Life is a text, right? Of course, papers are still assigned in the composition classroom, but not so many as there used to be. "We are living in a post-print world," one applicant explains, matter-of-factly.

17. As a boy, I would sit each summer morning by the mail slot that entered into our front sun porch. My home didn't contain books—my parents didn't read much—but I was so eager to digest written words that I would pore over anything that came by post. I lived with my mother and two sisters, so often it was women's magazines. Odd as it seems, I learned to read by digesting *Ladies' Home Journal, Redbook, Seventeen,* cover to

cover. Ads and articles. Later, I graduated to newsmagazines, *Time* and *Life*, and then young adult books. I was onto *Animal Farm* and Dickens before high school.

18. Reading and writing shaped my life, shaped my choices, showed me the way out of my childhood and into a world of possibility.

19. But that's just me. So what?

20. In truth, even I read far less these days. Unless you count e-mails and websites.

21. John Allemang lamented in the *Toronto Globe and Mail* some years back: "And yet, against the hopes of our parents and teachers and spouses and friends and sons and lovers, we don't read. Not the real stuff anyway. We are, as the experts like to say with a horrified sense of wonder, aliterate—able to read, and read well, but disinclined to do so. We can blame time and tiredness, changing technologies and altered priorities; still, a reluctance to read is not all that different from an inability."

22. My confession is nothing unique. I hear it over and over: "I have so little time. My eyes are tired at the end of the day. I pick up a book. I try to read. I put it down." The admission is almost always tinged with sadness.

23. Shortly after the job interviews in the deafening hotel room, I am visiting a Midwest MFA program to talk about writing to graduate students. Many of them use the post-print, visual-rhetoric approach to freshman English. "How is it working?" I ask.

24. "Not too well," one of them answers. "My students aren't really interested in watching films. I can't even get them to watch for ninety minutes a week."

25. Has it come to this: students too lazy to *watch?*

26. Back when people sat by the campfire, and not too long ago when people sat around a radio, there was great advantage to someone who could string a narrative out, make it last, fill the dark night air with words and words and words. The same was true of the novel. The literate class had many long evening hours to fill, and little to fill them with, so plots were protracted, and books lengthy.

27. Our world, like that hotel room in New York City, is under rapid reconstruction. We don't have long hours to fill; we hardly have time at all. We don't look forward to reading at night; we read on our little screens all day. Even movies seem too long. We live in an information maelstrom. Barraged from all sides. The constant noise of renovation.

28. The result, I sometimes think, is that our brains have been refurbished. We needed more room for storage: e-mail, voicemail, cable news, our investments, our diets, our health warnings, pins and passwords. Something had to go.

29. Turn the library into a media room. Reassign that frontal lobe. We are living in a post-print world.

30. Are you still reading?

31. You can stop now.

A Question from
BRIAN DOYLE

Mister Essay Writer Guy

Dear Mister Essay Writer Guy,

When you are clogged and stupid and weary, and you feel like every sentence you eke out is fatuous and literary and homiletic and sermonish and stentorian, and it feels like your stuff is stiff and officious, and you cannot ever imagine finding the verve and zest and fury and pop and silly of your work at its best, what do you do? Other than cold whiskey and hot showers and talking to children and small animals?

Yours,

Brian Doyle
Portland, Oregon

Dear Brian,

Clogged and stupid and weary pretty much sums up my artistic process, except for the occasional bouts of being fatuous, homiletic, stiff, and officious. Thank you for the reminder.

What do I do? Besides self-loathing?

Sometimes I just sit and draw pictures.

Despondently,

Mister Essay Writer Guy

Clogged and Stupid and Weary

My Writing Process

A Question from
LEE GUTKIND

Mister Essay Writer Guy

Dear Mister Essay Writer Guy,

Have I ever read anything you have written?

Sincerely,

Lee Gutkind
Pittsburgh, Pennsylvania

Lee,

Yes, you have now.

Mister Essay Writer Guy

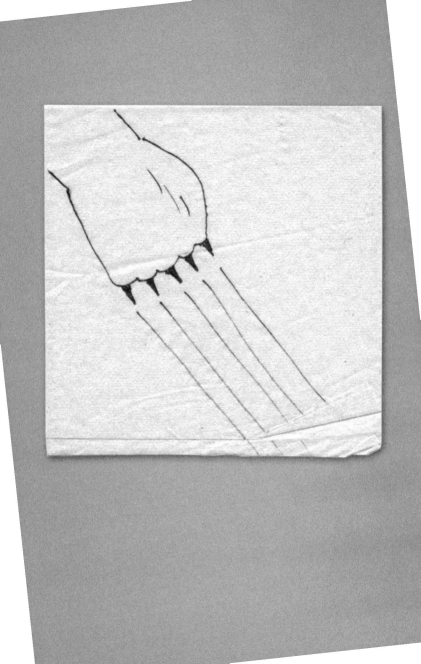

ACKNOWLEDGMENTS

Thanks Mom. Thanks wife and kid. Thanks Lisa, Carol, and Nami. Thanks to all of the wonderful authors who sent me questions. And thanks to all the polar bears everywhere. I'm your friend. Really.

ABOUT THE AUTHOR

(An essay constructed by entering "Dinty is . . ." into Google's search engine and extracting the sentences that were offered.)

Dinty is a newsboy whose fight to care for his ailing mother leads him into conflicts with the other boys on the street. Dinty is a former settlement in Humboldt County, California. A post office operated in Dinty during 1921. Dinty is the man. Dinty is the author of several books, including *Between Panic & Desire*. Dinty's is a pub that serves food and the food is average at best and overpriced at that. Dinty is a prize steer. Dinty is a collector, and would give three ears, if he had them, to get certain scarce items in the coin line. Dinty is a terrific guy at knowing that you don't have to play all the time, and that with nine people, in fact, it's really important that you don't play all the time. Dinty is a good, honest, intelligent, firm, fun man. But Dinty is not Dinky in any way. Dinty is a master of the short, provocative, helpful status update. While Dinty is a good dog, and will prove it to the public yet, he should have been placed second to Campbell's Little Dandy. Dinty is a nice person. Dinty is a person who has engendered respect both as a community member but more significantly to us as a family man. Dinty is a writer, teacher, graduate dissertation adviser, director of the Creative Writing Program at Ohio University. Dinty is following 0 people. Dinty is honest, charming, and disarming. He's got a great sense of humor. Dinty is a bit stingy with the beans.

INDEX

Gutenberg, Otto von
Daubenspeck, 19
Gutkind, Lee, 2, 186–88

H

Hemingway, Ernest
and bulls who march
proudly into the ring,
ready to die, 99
in Café Gijon, 91
opinion of Nelson
Algren, 147
vs. scholarly windbags, 91
Hippopotami,
disoriented, 178
Hollars, B. J., 86–88

J

Je ne sais quoi, 23
July, Miranda, 73

K

King Charles the Ninth, 81
cannibal friends of, 81
high school admissions
essay of, 81
Kitchen, Judith, 44–46

L

Laffer, Arthur, 38–39
Large intestine, 18
Lenney, Dinah, 106–10
Lincoln, Abe, 40–41
Literary agents, the desire to
throttle, 109
Lobes
frontal, 75–76, 181
occipital, 76
parietal, 76
temporal, 76
Lopate, Phillip, 2, 4–6, 118

M

Madden, Patrick, 82, 136–38
Magdalene, Mary, 20
Manny's Music Store, 66–67,
Marijuana abuse
while enjoying Road
Runner cartoons, 171
while escorting George
Plimpton, 61
while writing portions of
this book, [redacted]
Martone, Michael, 120–22
McLuhan, Marshall,
26–28, 32

Published in the United States by Ten Speed Press, an imprint of the Crown Publishing Group,
a division of Penguin Random House LLC, New York.
www.crownpublishing.com
www.tenspeed.com

Ten Speed Press and the Ten Speed Press colophon are registered trademarks of
Penguin Random House LLC.

Several of the essays in this work were previously published, some in very different form, in
Arts & Letters, Blip, Gulf Coast, Iron Horse Review, and Knee-Jerk. The author extends his sincere
gratitude to the editors of these journals.
"Of Bums" first published as a Roundtable in *Fourth Genre: Explorations in Nonfiction* (Vol. 11, No. 1,
Spring 2009), published by Michigan State University Press, East Lansing, MI.
"A Striped Essay" first published as "Of Striped Food and Polar Bears" in *TriQuarterly*, a publication
of Northwestern University, Chicago, IL.

Grateful acknowledgment is made to the following for permission to reprint previously published
material:
The Normal School: "Mr. Plimpton's Revenge," copyright © 2008 by Dinty W. Moore. First published
in *The Normal School* (Vol. 2, Issue 2). Reprinted by permission of *The Normal School*, a division of
the University Press, California State University, Fresno, CA.
The University of Nebraska Press: "Four Essential Tips for Telling the Truth in Personal Memoir
and Securing That Blockbuster Book Deal" from *Blurring the Boundaries: Explorations to the Fringes
of Nonfiction*, edited by B. J. Hollars, copyright © 2013 by the Board of Regents of the University of
Nebraska. Reprinted by permission of the University of Nebraska Press.
Writer's Digest Books: "Pulling Teeth" from *Crafting the Personal Essay: A Guide for Writing and
Publishing Creative Nonfiction*, by Dinty W. Moore, copyright © 2010 by Dinty W. Moore. Reprinted
by permission of Writer's Digest Books.

Library of Congress Cataloging-in-Publication Data

Moore, Dinty W., 1955-
 Dear mister essay writer guy : advice and confessions on writing, love, and cannibals /
Dinty W. Moore. — First edition.
 pages cm
 Includes bibliographical references and index.
 1. Essay—Authorship. 2. Creative nonfiction—Authorship. I. Title.
 PE1479.A88M67 2015
 808'.042—dc23
 2014041448

Hardcover ISBN: 978-1-60774-809-0
eBook ISBN: 978-1-60774-810-6

Printed in the United States of America

Design by Nami Kurita
Front cover image by iStock.com/elapela

10 9 8 7 6 5 4 3 2 1

First Edition